The Girl in the Song

The Girl in the Song

THE TRUE STORIES
BEHIND 50 ROCK CLASSICS

MICHAEL HEATLEY

CHICAGO
REVIEW
PRESS

An A Cappella Book

This edition published in 2011 by Chicago Review Press, Incorporated
First published in the United Kingdom in 2010 by Portico Books
An imprint of Anova Books Company Ltd
10 Southcombe Street, London W14 0RA

Chicago Review Press, Incorporated
814 North Franklin Street
Chicago, Illinois 60610
ISBN 978-1-56976-530-2
5 4 3 2 1

Cover design: Jonathan Hahn
Cover image: Anon (Getty Images)
Back cover image: Jane Birkin (Corbis)
Page 2: Pattie Boyd (Getty Images)

Reproduction by Rival Colour Ltd.
Printed and bound by 1010 Printing International Limited, China

Contents

Beware of Young Girls	6	Maybe I'm Amazed	70
Brilliant Disguise	8	Miss Amanda Jones	72
Carrie Anne	10	Moses	76
Chelsea Hotel No. 2	14	Mrs. Potter's Lullaby	78
Dear Prudence	16	My Sharona	80
Diana	18	Our House	82
Don't Think Twice, It's All Right	20	Peggy Sue	86
Every Breath You Take	24	Philadelphia Freedom	88
Femme Fatale	27	The Prettiest Star	92
Fire and Rain	30	Rikki Don't Lose That Number	96
Five Years Old	32	Rosanna	98
The Girl from Ipanema	34	Sara	100
Hearts and Bones	36	See Emily Play	102
Hey Negrita	38	She's Leaving Home	106
In the Air Tonight	42	Something / Layla	108
Irene Wilde	44	Suite: Judy Blue Eyes	112
It Ain't Me Babe	46	Suzanne	116
It Ain't Over 'til It's Over	50	Sweet Caroline	120
Je T'Aime (Moi Non Plus)	52	Sweet Child o' Mine	123
Jennifer Juniper	56	Sweetest Thing	127
Life on Mars?	58	Tiny Dancer	130
Lola	62	Turn Your Lights Down Low	132
Lovely Rita	64	Under My Thumb	134
Lucy in the Sky with Diamonds	66	Uptown Girl	138
Maggie May	68	Wonderwall	142

Beware of Young Girls

Dory Previn

Dory Previn gained moderate fame in the early 1970s as a painfully honest singer-songwriter, part of the new wave of introspective female performers that included Janis Ian. In 1975, when twenty-four-year-old Janis was winning a Grammy for her song "At Seventeen," Dory was turning fifty, a survivor of two serious nervous breakdowns induced by the men in her life.

The first, in 1965, was her delayed reaction to a traumatic childhood with her mentally unstable father. He had been gassed in World War I and suffered deep, violent periods of depression. Dorothy Langan (as Dory was born) had escaped into acting and singing and, in the 1950s, formed a personal and professional partnership with the composer André Previn, whom she met while working for MGM as a lyric writer. They wrote music for Hollywood and received two Oscar nominations for Best Original Song (one of them sung by Judy Garland). They were married in 1959.

Their last collaboration was on five songs for the 1967 film *Valley of the Dolls*. André began to accept work with orchestras around the world, but Dory's fear of flying prevented her from accompanying her husband. It was at the start of his tenure as conductor of the London Symphony Orchestra in 1968 that André began an affair with Mia Farrow, ex-wife of Frank Sinatra. Mia was twenty-four, nineteen years younger than Dory and fifteen years younger than her husband. Dory's discovery in early 1969 that Mia was pregnant ended her marriage to André and precipitated her second, more serious breakdown. She was institutionalized for a second time and received electroconvulsive therapy for her condition.

> Beware of young girls who come to the door
> Wistful and pale, of twenty and four
> Delivering daisies with delicate hands

As she emerged from her trauma and returned to work, Dory found that her songwriting was contributing to her therapy and becoming more introspective. An early product of this soul-searching was 1970's "Beware of Young Girls." The musical arrangement and lyrics have a lightness of touch through which her bitter sense of betrayal pours.

André and Mia married in due course, raising a family of six natural and adopted children and remaining on good terms after they divorced in 1979. In 1980 Farrow began dating film director Woody Allen, a mere nine years her senior. That relationship fell apart very publicly in 1992 when Farrow discovered Allen's affair with Soon-Yi Previn, one of the children adopted by Mia and André, and thirty-five years Allen's junior.

In 1997, Woody and Soon-Yi married. Mia refused to see Soon-Yi

Mia Farrow, looking suitably "wistful and pale," in 1964.

again, and that year Farrow published an autobiography in which she belatedly apologized to Dory. Dory collaborated with André again in 1997, for the first time since 1967, on a seventeen minute piece for orchestra and soprano, entitled *The Magic Number*.

She seems at last to be at peace with herself: "The world has delved into my life—it knows all my secrets. That's what I'm here for." As for being at peace with Mia, she was asked in 2008 if she knew whether her betrayer had ever heard "Beware of Young Girls." "With her ego? Of course she did. She's probably got the record framed in the bathroom!"

DORY PREVIN found commercial music success after spending years writing songs for motion pictures. It was after this she used her wit and sense of irony to release songs to which many women could relate. "Beware of Young Girls" was released on Previn's second LP, *On My Way to Where*, her first effort having been released under her maiden name of Langan, and came out some twelve years earlier. She went on to release no less than six more LPs before 1976. The often controversial nature of her material prevented Dory Previn from reaching the heights of commercial acceptance that many of her contemporaries achieved, but she did not perform for the recognition, rather the catharsis.

Brilliant Disguise
Bruce Springsteen

Julianne Phillips and Bruce Springsteen seemed an ideal celebrity couple. She was a model and an actress, described as a "perfect ten package"; eleven years her senior, he was one of the most successful rock stars in the world, with a hard-earned reputation as a barnstorming live performer.

Before they actually met in person, Springsteen had already seen Phillips in promotional videos and in two TV movies, and she was undoubtedly aware of "The Boss," one of America's major rock stars. They were introduced in Los Angeles by his booking agent in October 1984. Discovering shared enthusiasms for working out and 1950s rock 'n' roll, they became close and were married in May 1985 in Phillips's hometown of Lake Oswego, Oregon.

Springsteen's people tried hard to maintain secrecy, but news of the wedding leaked to the media via Julianne's parents. This resulted in the ceremony being brought forward to shortly after midnight on May 13 to throw off reporters and paparazzi. The small town became a media circus for the reception two days later, with a swarm of helicopters in attendance. This led Springsteen to comment ruefully, "I do not believe or comprehend the world that I live in."

Julianne Phillips was branded the "perfect ten package" by her modeling agency.

At a gig shortly after their wedding, Springsteen would sing Elvis Presley's "Can't Help Falling in Love" onstage while gazing at an adoring Phillips, who stood in the wings. By the time of his *Tunnel of Love* album two years later, rumors that all was not well in the marriage were lent credence by the nature of the songs, in particular "Brilliant Disguise," with its images of masks, role-playing, mutual suspicion, and betrayal.

> So tell me what I see when I look in your eyes
> Is that you baby or just a brilliant disguise
> I want to know if it's you I don't trust
> Cause I damn sure don't trust myself

Springsteen has rarely spoken about what went wrong in the marriage, although he has confessed to his own failings: "I didn't really know how to be a husband. She was a terrific person, but I just didn't know how to do it." Later, he confided that "I found I'd gotten very good at my job and, because I was good at my job, for some reason I thought I was capable of a lot of other things, like relationships."

The couple agreed to a trial separation during Springsteen's Tunnel of Love tour in 1988. They filed for divorce in August of that year, and the settlement was finalized the following March. By then, Bruce's relationship with backing singer Patti Scialfa was common knowledge; he married her two years later.

As part of the divorce settlement Phillips agreed not to talk in public about her relationship with Springsteen. Julianne went on to pursue a career in acting, appearing in the movie *Fletch Lives* and the TV drama *Sisters*. Since 1997 she has lived a low-profile life in Los Angeles.

BRUCE SPRINGSTEEN was already a global superstar by the time he released "Brilliant Disguise" in 1987; his breakthrough album, *Born to Run*, had secured his position as a major force in American rock twelve years earlier, while 1984's *Born in the U.S.A.* saw him at his bombastic best.

He drew back from that successful style for "Brilliant Disguise," which nevertheless hit #5 on the Billboard Hot 100, while the album *Tunnel of Love* topped the album charts. Though a difficult time for Springsteen personally, the period was perhaps his most successful professionally, as *Tunnel* was his sixth consecutive Top 5 LP.

That run continued into the twenty-first century, the only blip coming in 1995 with the commercially disappointing *The Ghost of Tom Joad*. Still, with seven #1 albums and now into his sixties, Springsteen continues to show why he's "The Boss."

Carrie Anne

The Hollies

Marianne Faithfull was the daughter of an Austro-Hungarian baroness, while her great uncle, Baron Leopold von Sascher-Masoch, developed the theory of "masochism." She was seventeen and not long out of convent school when she attended a party on Wimpole Street in London's West End. She was escorted by boyfriend John Dunbar, a painter and fulcrum of the city's avant-garde scene. Also present were Rolling Stones Mick Jagger and Keith Richards with their manager, Andrew Loog Oldham. Marianne made quite an impact on Oldham; he recalled her "sexy body and virginal smile ... and what a name—Marianne Faithfull! You can't make up a better name than that." Adding Faithfull to his roster of artists, Oldham persuaded Jagger and Richards to write a song, "As Tears Go By," for her. After it became her first hit single in summer 1964, she was sent on a typical mid-1960s promotional package tour featuring a diverse roster of acts, including Mancunian hitmakers the Hollies.

Although she struck up a friendship with singer-guitarist Graham Nash, whom she describes as one of the "nice people," it was lead singer Allan Clarke with whom she had a brief fling. Clarke was married at the time but Marianne recalled: "If it felt good you did it. It would have been hypocritical not to sleep with someone simply because he or she was involved with someone else!"

Speaking in 2007, Marianne recalled the breakneck speed at which her career had been launched: "I was whisked off and before I knew what was going on I had a record in the charts and I was on tour with the Hollies.... At eighteen I had a baby, then at nineteen I ran off with Mick. When I was twenty-four, it all fell apart. I realised I couldn't deal with it."

In May 1967, the Hollies released "Carrie Anne," one of their best-loved singles, composed by Clarke, Nash, and lead guitarist Tony Hicks. It was not until 1995 that Nash revealed the identity of Carrie Anne. Interviewed for the documentary TV series *The History of Rock 'n' Roll*, he stated that he had written the song for Marianne Faithfull but was "too shy" to use her real name.

Shortly afterwards she left Dunbar and embarked on a relationship

Marianne Faithfull, photographed in January 1965, following the success of her first single, "As Tears Go By." Still a teenager, she was about to be "swerved off course."

with Mick Jagger, having first slept with fellow Rolling Stones Brian Jones and Keith Richards. Drug use became the norm for Marianne, who described her life at this time as being "swerved off course." In February 1967, she was among those arrested at Richards's house in a notorious police raid. She refers to the pivotal moment as "that dreadful drugs bust." Found wearing only a bearskin rug, Faithfull was later demonized: "It destroyed me. To be a male drug addict and to act like that is always enhancing and glamorising. A woman in that situation becomes a slut and a bad mother."

By 1970, Marianne had split with Jagger. She was a heroin addict and had attempted suicide, which led to her losing custody of her son. Much of the following decade was spent in a personal hell of addiction and homelessness. She re-emerged in 1979 with the acclaimed LP *Broken English* and resumed the acting career which had begun on the London stage in 1967. Her most recent album, *Easy Come, Easy Go*, was released in 2008. Having survived breast cancer to become something of a national treasure in Britain, she remains realistic about her status: "Most kids would say, 'This woman? I don't want to make those mistakes!' I'm sort of an anti–role model."

THE HOLLIES were Manchester's highest-flying 1960s beat group. Their sound was based around the breathtaking vocal blend of singer Allan Clarke and guitarists Tony Hicks and Graham Nash who — under the communal pseudonym "L. Ransford"—also composed many of their hits from 1963 to 1968. Yet it was a nonoriginal "Look Through Any Window," that broke out the Hollies in the U.S. in 1966. More reliant on outside writers after Nash left to form Crosby, Stills & Nash, the band registered hits with "The Air That I Breathe"—and, as late as 1983, a reworking of "Stop! In the Name of Love." Moreover, via its use in a TV commercial, a re-release of 1969's "He Ain't Heavy (He's My Brother)" was a U.K. #1 in 1988. Clarke retired, but Hicks and drummer Bobby Elliott continued into the new millennium.

Faithfull had only just left school when her pop career took off—her mother's house in Reading served as the backdrop for this 1964 publicity shot.

Chelsea Hotel No. 2
Leonard Cohen

The Chelsea Hotel would soon celebrate a century in existence and was well on the way to becoming the best-known flophouse in rock 'n' roll when Leonard Cohen immortalized it in song. The structure, the tallest building in New York City until 1884, is three-quarters occupied by permanent residents. Dylan Thomas was taken from there breathing his last in 1953, while another Dylan, Bob, penned "Sad-Eyed Lady of the Lowlands" within its walls.

Canadian poet-turned-troubadour Cohen loved the hotel: "It's one of those hotels that have everything that I love so well.... I love hotels to which, at 4 a.m., you can bring along a midget, a bear and four ladies, drag them to your room and no one cares about it at all."

Cohen has admitted that he wrote this song about a brief affair he had with firebrand singer Janis Joplin, although since her death he has come to regret linking her name with the song. In a 1994 BBC radio interview, Cohen referred to it as "the sole indiscretion in my professional life."

Janice Joplin wasn't overly impressed by Cohen when she first encountered him in the elevator of the Chelsea Hotel.

The raspy-voiced Joplin was born in Texas in 1943; she first came to fame in San Francisco in 1966 fronting Big Brother and the Holding Company. An incendiary performance at the Monterey Pop Festival in 1967 alongside Hendrix catapulted her to overnight fame. *Time* magazine called Joplin "probably the most powerful singer to emerge from the white rock movement.[1] But a history of drug and alcohol abuse mixed with a healthy helping of self-loathing (she had been unceasingly tormented at school about her lack of looks) would prove to be Joplin's undoing. She appeared at Woodstock in 1969 with new backing group the Kozmic Blues Band, but she was so out of it that she wasn't included in the movie.

The pair of unlikely rock stars made even less likely bedfellows. Legend has it they first met in an elevator, Joplin having entered and expressed disappointment it wasn't Kris Kristofferson in the lift. Nevertheless they consummated their relationship, not then and there but on "the unmade bed" in room 104.

> You told me again you preferred handsome men
> But for me you would make an exception

In 1971 Janis Joplin topped the album charts with *Pearl* and the singles chart with "Me and Bobby McGee"—ironically penned by her idol, Kris Kristofferson—but she had sadly died the previous year from a heroin overdose. Her place of death was another hotel, the Landmark in Hollywood.

When Cohen wrote his eulogy to her in 1971, he was at pains to paint the relationship as brief and relatively meaningless.

Since Cohen penned "Chelsea Hotel No. 2," Sid Vicious, bass player of the Sex Pistols, wrote a more grisly chapter in the hotel's history by murdering girlfriend Nancy Spungen in the bathroom of nearby suite number 100 in October 1978.

LEONARD COHEN wrote "Chelsea Hotel No. 2" in 1971. He was assisted by Ron Cornelius, a guitarist who served as Cohen's bandleader for four albums. The song was apparently penned on a transatlantic flight from the U.S. to Shannon, Ireland.

The song was first played live in London in 1972 but would not be recorded until 1974's *New Skin for the Old Ceremony* album. Its fame was cemented when just fifteen months later it appeared on his *Greatest Hits*, a must for all fans of bedsitter imagery, aligning it with the tried and trusted likes of "Suzanne" and "So Long Marianne." A different version of the song with gentler lyrics was recorded for Tony Palmer's *Bird on a Wire* documentary, but it is unclear if this was Chelsea Hotel No. 1 or merely a first draft.

Dear Prudence
The Beatles

Prudence Farrow was overjoyed to be accepted for a two-month Transcendental Meditation course at Maharishi Mahesh Yogi's ashram at Rishikesh, India. "I'd been meditating since 1966 and had tried to get on the course in 1967, so it was a dream come true for me," she recalled. Arriving in February 1968 with actress and elder sister Mia, she discovered that among her fellow students were the Beatles, whose spiritual quest had also led them to India.

Failing to heed the Indian holy man's warning about the dangers of overdoing the practice, twenty-year-old Prudence spent long hours meditating alone in her chalet. John Lennon remembered that, "All the people around her were very worried because she was going insane. So we sang to her.... They selected me and George to try and bring her out because she would trust us. She went completely mental. If she'd been in the West they would have put her away. We got her out of the house. She'd been locked in for three weeks and wouldn't come out, trying to reach God quicker than anybody else. That was the competition in

Prudence Farrow (far left) at Maharishi Mahesh Yogi's ashram in Rishikesh in February 1968. Alongside her are Ringo Starr, his wife Maureen Starkey, and Jane Asher.

Maharishi's camp: who was going to get cosmic first." Prudence remembered events differently. "Being on that course was more important to me than anything in the world. I was very focused on getting in as much meditation as possible, so that I could gain enough experience to teach it myself. I knew that I must have stuck out because I would always rush straight back to my room after lectures and meals so that I could meditate. John, George and Paul would all want to sit around jamming and having a good time and I'd be flying into my room. They were all serious about what they were doing but they just weren't as fanatical as me."

"Dear Prudence" was composed by Lennon and his fellow Beatles in India. Its lyric aimed to tempt Prudence out by appealing to her inner child with lines like: "The clouds will be a daisy chain, so let me see you smile again," and the refrain "Won't you come out to play?" References to beauties of nature—the sun, the sky, and birds singing—reflected the camp's idyllic setting at the foothills of the Himalayas.

According to Paul McCartney, "John sang it to her outside her door with his guitar." Prudence, however, has no recollection of being serenaded by Lennon. "At the end of the course, just as they were leaving, George mentioned that they had written a song about me but I didn't hear it until it came out on the album. I was flattered. It was a beautiful thing to have done."

California resident Prudence went on to work in film as a production assistant and art-department coordinator. She conceived and co-produced the 1994 movie *Widow's Peak*. She also gained qualifications in South & South East Asian studies from the University of Berkeley. While John Lennon denounced the Maharishi shortly before leaving Rishikesh, following allegations that the guru had made a pass at Mia, Prudence's devotion to Transcendental Meditation remained as strong as ever; she went on to teach the discipline for more than thirty-five years.

THE BEATLES included "Dear Prudence" on their self-titled ninth British LP, also known as *The White Album*. It was never released as a single, but its parent topped the charts across the world, something that had become the norm for the Beatles throughout the decade. It was their biggest-selling album in America, going platinum an incredible nineteen times. Their next album, *Yellow Submarine*, paled in comparison, but still easily made the Top 3 in both the U.K. and U.S.

Diana
Paul Anka

Is this the original teenage crush? "Diana" is the template for songs of unrequited adolescent yearning, which have been the basis of the pop-hit industry ever since. It has sold more than twenty million copies worldwide and all because, in 1956, the fifteen-year-old Anka became infatuated with an eighteen-year-old friend from his local church in Ottawa. Her name was Diana Ayoub.

> I'm so young and you're so old
> This, my darling, I've been told

A "mature" Anka, age eighteen, prepares for his Las Vegas debut at the Sahara Hotel.

Diana was just not interested. As she recalled years later, "My girlfriend said he was in love with me and I told her, 'Don't be ridiculous, he's our friend.'" But Paul had it bad, and when he finally summoned the nerve to show Diana his new song he only played the piano part, too shy to sing the words declaring his love. Instead he used to sing it at other people's parties, hoping word would get back to Diana.

He took to calling on the Ayoub household on one pretext or another morning, noon, and night. But if Diana's father was fed up with this persistent intrusion, it was nothing compared to the disruption the family faced when the song became a huge international hit the following year.

Everyone wanted to know who the Diana in the song was. Although at first she enjoyed the attention and gave interviews, it soon became a nightmare. "I had reporters waiting for me when I graduated from high school," she says. "Guys wouldn't ask me out because their picture would be in the newspaper the next day." On one occasion Mr. Ayoub found an abandoned set of stepladders beneath his daughter's bedroom window.

Anka recorded "Diana" in New York and never moved back to his home city. Indeed, after a bad local review of a concert in Ottawa in 1981, he refused even to perform there again until 2002. Eventually he relocated to Los Angeles, where in 1986 he cowrote with Michael Jackson the song which would become the latter's epitaph in 2009—"This Is It." A year after working with Anka, Jackson would rework the theme of unreciprocated attraction in his hit "Dirty Diana."

For Diana Ayoub, normal existence became impossible in the wake of the song's success. She was spied on and hounded by the press, pestered constantly by reporters looking for personal details about her or Paul. At last the limelight faded, and she was able to get on with ordinary life.

Diana stayed in Ottawa, married, raised a family, and worked, becoming a manager of a wholesale clothing warehouse, Divine Liquidation. She is now retired, and perhaps able to smile at last about the bashful young man who made his fortune singing about her.

PAUL ANKA, the Canadian singer-songwriter, actor, and all-around entertainer, carved out a career spanning five decades, metamorphosing from teen heart-throb to seasoned performer in order to maintain and even grow his popularity over time.

It was his #1 debut "Diana" that introduced Anka to the public in 1957 and propelled him into the spotlight. He went on to have success both as a singer and a songwriter, penning the English lyrics to "My Way," the song that would define the career of Frank Sinatra, as well as Tom Jones's classic, "She's a Lady."

Don't Think Twice, It's All Right

Bob Dylan

While it was written a year earlier, "Don't Think Twice, It's All Right" was released in 1963, a pivotal year for pop with Bob Dylan and the Beatles both breaking though into the mainstream. It was also a year of personal pain for Dylan as Suze Rotolo, his muse and the woman pictured cuddling up to him in the street on the cover of his second album, *The Freewheelin' Bob Dylan*, had left him.

The pair had met in the spring of 1961, after she saw him performing in a Greenwich Village club. They met again a few weeks later. "Right from the start I couldn't take my eyes off her," Dylan wrote in his autobiography, *Chronicles*. "She was the most erotic thing I'd ever seen. She was fair-skinned and golden-haired, full-blood Italian.... We started talking and my head started to spin.... She was just my type."

An acquaintance described them as "like two innocent children, falling in love," but when Dylan recorded his first album later in 1961, Suze began to realize that he was about to be successful and that the unquestioning loyalty he demanded would mean she could not enjoy a life of her own. "I certainly felt that, as his girlfriend, I disappeared and became a nonentity. Even if he didn't see me that way, that's what happened. That was always a struggle."

Susan Elizabeth Rotolo came from a family with strong left-wing connections; both parents, the children of Italian immigrants, were members of the American Communist Party, and she described herself as being a "red diaper baby"—a child of communists during the McCarthy Era.

Dylan acknowledged her influence when he told an interviewer, "Suze was into this equality-freedom thing long before I was. I checked out the songs with her." She worked as a secretary for the Congress on Racial Equality and was associated with protests against the travel ban against Cuba. Through her Dylan would learn much about the civil rights situation and the problems faced by black people. The folk music and civil rights movements were very much interlinked.

After six months of living with Dylan, Rotolo decided to travel to Italy with her mother and stepfather (her father died when she was fourteen) to study art at the University of Perugia. Dylan missed her and wrote long letters, hoping she would return soon to New York. She postponed her

Suze Rotolo and Dylan in 1961, before the release of his first album. At this time Rotolo began to feel sidelined: "As his girlfriend, I disappeared and became a nonentity."

turn several times, finally coming back in January 1963. Critics have connected the intense love songs expressing longing and loss on *Freewheelin'* to Dylan's fraught relationship with Rotolo, particularly "Don't Think Twice, It's All Right."

"One Too Many Mornings" and "Tomorrow Is a Long Time" are also songs of parting and loss written while she was away, while another *Freewheelin'* track, "Down the Highway," contains a direct mention of Rotolo in Perugia:

> My baby took my heart from me
> She packed it all up in a suitcase
> Lord, she took it away to Italy, Italy

Dylan traveled to England in late 1962, and then to Italy, unaware that Suze was already en route to New York. When Dylan returned to New York in mid-January 1963, he persuaded her to move in to his apartment on West Fourth Street. The *Freewheelin'* cover photograph was taken a few weeks later by Columbia staff photographer Don Hunstein at the corner of Jones Street and West Fourth Street in Greenwich Village,

BOB DYLAN has become one of America's leading artists over the last fifty years, blending commercial and critical success with his music that draws on countless genres. "Don't Think Twice, It's All Right" featured on his second LP, *The Freewheelin' Bob Dylan*. It wasn't released as a single, but the album, which included some of his most celebrated compositions, topped the chart in the U.K.

Dylan has continued to make his mark not only in American music but also in culture; his lyrics and songs have managed to defy time, as was proved in 2009 when *Together Through Life* returned him to the pinnacle of the U.S. album charts for the fifth time. He has maintained his reputation as one of America's greatest singer-songwriters, his albums consistently charting for more than four decades.

New York City, just a few yards away from the apartment where the couple lived.

The influence of Bertolt Brecht on Dylan's songwriting and performing has been acknowledged as stemming from Suze's participation in Brechtian theater. She invited him to a rehearsal of George Tabori's *Brecht on Brecht* at the Sheridan Square Playhouse, and in *Chronicles* he describes how hearing the performance of Kurt Weill's "Pirate Jenny" provoked a fundamental change in his approach to songwriting. Dylan's interest in painting can also be traced back to his relationship with Rotolo.

In the *Freewheelin'* sleeve notes, Dylan comments, "It isn't a love song. It's a statement that maybe you can say to make yourself feel better. It's as if you were talking to yourself."

Dylan biographer Howard Sounes commented: "The greatness of the song was in the cleverness of the language. The phrase 'Don't think twice, it's all right' could be snarled, sung with resignation, or delivered with an ambiguous mixture of bitterness and regret. Seldom has the contradictory emotions of a thwarted lover been so well expressed and the song transcends the autobiographical origins of Dylan's pain."

In May 1963, Dylan performed with Joan Baez at the Monterey Folk Festival, where she joined him on stage in a duet of a new Dylan song, "With God on Our Side." The performance marked the beginning of a romantic relationship between Baez and Dylan. Suze Rotolo put distance between herself and Dylan by moving to Cuba in mid-1964, breaking the U.S. travel embargo despite its being illegal to do so.

In 1970 she married Enzo Bartoliocci, whom she had met during her student days in Perugia. They have one son, Luca, who is a guitar maker in New York. In Dylanologist Michael Gray's words, "In the years after their demise as an item, Rotolo retained Dylan's respect by her determined silence and her absolute refusal to give interviews."

Yet this ended relatively recently when she was interviewed in a 2004 TV documentary produced by New York PBS Channel 13 and the *New York Daily News*. That same November, she appeared at the Experience Music Project on a panel discussing Dylan's early days in Greenwich Village. Rotolo also appeared in Martin Scorsese's film *No Direction Home*, a documentary focusing on Dylan's early career from 1961 to 1966.

Suze Rotolo's *A Freewheelin' Time: A Memoir of Greenwich Village in the Sixties* was published by Broadway Books in 2008 and included accounts of her time with Dylan.

Every Breath You Take
The Police

Gordon Sumner and Frances Tomelty married in 1976 after knowing each other for two years. They met on the set of a rock musical called *Rock Nativity*; she was the Virgin Mary, he played in the band.

Born in Belfast in 1948, the daughter of actor Joseph Tomelty, Frances was an established actress. A long-distance relationship resulted and bassist-vocalist Sumner, known as Sting to his friends due to the design of a favorite striped sweater, decided to move down to London from his native Newcastle, having put his teaching career on hold. Her earnings kept their household afloat as Sting tried to make his band, Last Exit, a success.

When this failed he formed the Police and successfully jumped on the late-1970s postpunk bandwagon, performing the songs he wrote with energy that belied the three musicians' relative maturity.

The first of Gordon and Frances's two children, Joseph, was born in November 1976. But shortly after the release of the fourth Police album, *Ghost in the Machine*, and the birth of their second child, Kate, in April 1982, Sting left his six-year marriage and moved in with their neighbor—Trudie Styler, also an actress—who would become his second wife. But this did not stop Sting from referring to "my awful separation from my wife ... Frances Tomelty," nor using her as the inspiration for his most successful song.

"Every Breath You Take" was described by the *Times* as "a couple of bars' worth of music, a strong central thought and two minutes with a rhyming dictionary."

> Every breath you take
> Every move you make
> I'll be watching you

But after several years of trying, Sting had created that perfect paradox: a pop song that worked on more than one level. Many of those who bought "Every Breath You Take" considered it a hymn of devotion, the singer following in his loved one's footsteps like a faithful hound. But a scan of the lyrics (included in a Police album package for the first time)

"I'll be watching you." Tomelty and Sting in 1982, the year he left her for Trudie Styler.

suggested otherwise. Its writer described it as "a song of experience, about jealousy and possession ... a sinister, evil song veiled in a romantic setting." He was always amused when fans chose it as their wedding song.

When asked why he appears angry in the music video he told BBC Radio 2, "I think the song is very, very sinister and ugly and people have misinterpreted it as being a gentle, little love song."

"Every Breath" had been written in idyllic surroundings—the Jamaican hideaway of Golden Eye, at the same desk where 007's creator Ian Fleming had plotted and planned James Bond's next move.

By March 1984, Frances Tomelty and Sting had divorced. The petition was granted on the grounds that Frances and Sting had not lived together for nearly two years. "I'm happy everything has gone through," she told reporters at the time. "It's been done amicably. Now I am concentrating on my career."

And that she has. The irony of the situation is that Tomelty's separation from Sting led to her becoming an even more accomplished actress, while Styler, who was working as an actress for the Royal Shakespeare Company (RSC) in London, found her leading roles drying up. Bizarrely, as Styler was exiting the RSC, Tomelty was taking on more roles for the company and moved to work at the home theatre in Stratford. Through the 1980s, she worked with some of British theater's leading directors. "I was thrilled when I went there. I think I was probably quite good when I left but not when I was actually learning. In the first couple of years, I thought: 'Everybody knows more than I do,' working with drama school-trained actors."

She has worked onstage and in film and television. In 2005 while in Dublin to narrate a symphonic work by Bobby Lamb, *The Company of Lir*, she told Dublin's *Sunday Independent*, "I'm not famous any more and I've worked quite hard [at that]. I mean, I haven't given an interview for God knows how long. My choice was to become as boring as I possibly could so I gave a series of extremely dull interviews during which I could see journalists dropping off and then people stopped asking.

"You don't have to be famous. I'm not asked now but at a time when I was, I didn't show up; I didn't wear the clothes; I didn't go to the parties. So after a while one ceases to be [of interest]; you have to work quite hard to stay famous."

THE POLICE brought their energetic, reggae-infused rock to the masses in the 1970s and 1980s, led by frontman Sting. Though only active for seven years and five albums, their impact was undeniable, Sting later enjoying success as a solo artist. With the Police's members having dispersed to follow individual projects for the previous eighteen months, "Every Breath You Take" showed the group had not yet broken up. It was a transatlantic chart topper, their first U.S. #1 and their fifth at home in the U.K. American success was particularly long-lived at eight weeks, making it a close second to "Hey Jude" as the most enduring chart topper from a British band. It was also *Billboard* magazine's bestselling single of the year. Less than a year after the single, the group disbanded, but they re-formed to tour in 2007. As a footnote, the song inspired Michael Stipe of REM to write another classic. "It was beautiful and creepy. So I wanted to write a song ('Losing My Religion') that was better."

THE POLICE

EVERY BREATH YOU TAKE

Femme Fatale
The Velvet Underground

The 1960s bohemian scene in America was personified by one man— Andy Warhol. The artist had a hand in countless projects including film and music. It was the latter that found him involved with the Velvet Underground.

He played a major role in the band's formation and designed the iconic "banana" cover of their first album, *The Velvet Underground & Nico*, which stands alongside *Sgt. Pepper's Lonely Hearts Club Band* as 1967's most influential recording.

Edie Sedgwick was one of Warhol's famous "Superstars," a group of liberal and eccentric women who characterized bohemia. As the public faces of his work, the Superstars lived the carefree life of free love at the artist's Factory, his studio in midtown Manhattan.

California-born Sedgwick was one of the original "It" girls, and quickly took the attention of Warhol after they met in early 1965. This gathered a lot of media attention, and when Warhol became the Velvet Underground's manager in 1965, he wanted a song befitting of his muse.

"Andy said I should write a song about Edie Sedgwick," Velvet's frontman Lou Reed recalls. "I said 'Like what?' And he said 'Oh, don't you think she's a femme fatale, Lou?' So I wrote 'Femme Fatale.'"

The lyrics left little to the imagination as to Sedgwick's allure to the opposite sex. It painted her as a temptress, the object of many men's affections but ultimately unobtainable:

> 'Cause everybody knows
> (She's a femme fatale)
> The things she does to please
> (She's a femme fatale)
> She's just a little tease

Sedgwick starred in a number of Warhol's avant-garde films, including *Poor Little Rich Girl* and *Beauty No. 2*, which, while not commercially successful, made a name for her in the right circles.

She eventually left Warhol's circle in 1966, taking up residence

Andy Warhol was fascinated by Sedgwick, a Californian heiress and socialite on the New York art scene. Warhol intended to crown her the queen of his Factory of "Superstars."

in the renowned counterculture hangout the Chelsea Hotel in New York City. It was here that she briefly linked up with Bob Dylan. There were even plans for Sedgwick to be represented by Dylan's manager Albert Grossman. Rumors of a relationship with Dylan were common currency but never substantiated, although she did date Dylan's friend Bob Neuwirth until early in 1967 when he broke off the relationship. The constant drug abuse and erratic behavior proved too much.

She persevered with her acting career and auditioned for Norman Mailer's play *The Deer Park*. Mailer thought she "wasn't very good." In April 1967 she began shooting underground movie *Ciao! Manhattan* a film which would take another five years to finish.

Sedgwick's last years were not happy ones; her family moved her back to California after her health detriorated and she was in and out of psychiatric institutions amid spiraling drug problems. A rare high point was marriage to a fellow patient, Michael Post.

Her life of excess came to a tragic end in 1971, after attending a fashion show at the Santa Barbara Museum. At the after-show party she was upset by a woman who told her her marriage would fail. She died in her sleep that night at the apartment she shared with Post; the coroner ruled Sedgwick's death as "undetermined/accident/suicide." The femme fatale's life had come to a fatal stop at just twenty-eight.

THE VELVET UNDERGROUND never enjoyed substantial chart success during their lifetime, but their influence on rock 'n' roll and its future artists has become their legacy. "Femme Fatale" was included in their debut album, *The Velvet Underground & Nico*, which only managed #171 in the U.S. on its release in 1967. The song was never released as a single. Despite the lack of units shifted at the time, members of the group went on to have successful solo careers, particularly lead singer and songwriter Lou Reed, who continued to influence many more artists in the next forty years. Other notable members included German singer Nico and Welsh bassist-viola player John Cale.

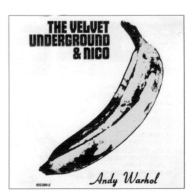

Fire and Rain

James Taylor

After a false start on the Beatles' Apple label, American singer-songwriter Taylor broke through with the 1970 album *Sweet Baby James*, on which "Fire and Rain" was the standout track. The first verse is a eulogy for his friend Suzanne Schnerr, a girl from Long Island whom Taylor had encountered in New York when she was a teenager and who later committed suicide. Taylor explained that she died suddenly and that friends at home, concerned it might distract Taylor from his big break with Apple, had kept the tragic news from him. He only found out some time later.

> Just yesterday morning they let me know you were gone
> Suzanne the plans they made put an end to you

Taylor's former heroin addiction resurfaced, and he returned to the U.S. for treatment. The second verse was written in a hospital room in Manhattan with his "body aching and ... time at hand." James completed the song in the Austin Riggs Hospital in Stockbridge, Massachusetts. The electroshock therapy he underwent is apparently the "fire" of the song's title.

The reference to flying machines ("Sweet dreams and flying machines in pieces on the ground") is to his first group, the Flying Machine, in which he first met longtime guitarist Danny "Kootch" Kortchmar. It was an acknowledgment of Taylor's despair at the failure of this early band, with which he began playing in public around Greenwich Village before moving to London in an unsuccessful attempt to shake his drug habit.

Many listeners took the lyrics literally, and rumors began to circulate that Suzanne Schnerr was Taylor's girlfriend and had died in a plane crash en route to visit him. Not so, as he explained directly to *Rolling Stone* in 1972. "The first verse is about my reactions to the death of a friend. The second verse is about my arrival in this country with a monkey on my back, and there Jesus is an expression of my desperation in trying to get through the time when my body was aching and the time was at hand when I had to do it.... And the third verse of that song refers to my recuperation in Austin Riggs which lasted about five months."

Taylor has revealed little of Suzanne Schnerr over the years, but told biographer Timothy White that "I knew Suzanne well in New York, and we used to hang out together and we used to get high together; I think she came from Long Island. She was a kid, like all of us.

"[Suzanne] committed suicide sometime later while I was over in London. At the time I was living with Margaret [Corey], and Richard [Corey] was around a lot, and so was Joel O'Brien. All three of them were really close to Suzie Schnerr. But Richard and Joel and Margaret were excited for me having this record deal and making this album, and when Suzie killed herself they decided not to tell me about it until later because they didn't want to shake me up.

"I didn't find out until some six months after it happened. That's why the 'They let me know you were gone' line came up. And I always felt rather bad about the line, 'The plans they made put an end to you,' because 'they' only meant 'ye gods,' or basically 'the Fates.' I never knew her folks but I always wondered whether her folks would hear that and wonder whether it was about them."

"Fire and Rain" came to define Taylor's signature sound, and he usually includes it in all of his live shows.

JAMES TAYLOR used a troubled personal life to help him become a Grammy-winning singer-songwriter, his songs selling in the millions. "Fire and Rain" was Taylor's second Warner Brothers single after the slow start of "Carolina in My Mind"; his debut effort only reached #67 in the U.S.

"Fire and Rain" quickly rose to #3 on the Billboard Hot 100 when released as a single and attracted an immediate cover by Anne Murray. One year later he reached the top of the charts with his version of Carole King's "You've Got a Friend." He would not look back.

He has continued to release LPs to this day, and they rarely chart outside the Billboard Top 40. His most famous albums have all been re-released, making his emotive, self-penned songs as popular as they were thirty years ago.

Five Years Old
Loudon Wainwright III

The word "dynasty" gets bandied about whenever Wainwrights are mentioned these days. Popular music is so relatively young, even now, that it's still a novelty when children follow their parents into the business. Rufus and Martha Wainwright are two such children. Unlike many sons and daughters of famous pop parents, however, their own achievements already outweigh those of their illustrious mom and dad.

Mother Kate McGarrigle was herself part of a family business as one half of a duo with her sister Anna. The pair were leading lights in the Canadian folk-music scene of the early 1970s when Kate met Loudon Wainwright III, a successful singer-songwriter with a penchant for wistful, self-deprecating humor that often masked a sadder story.

Rufus was born in 1973 and Martha three years later, but by 1977 Loudon and Kate had separated. He had already written songs about both new arrivals: "Rufus Is a Tit Man" is a song of jealousy about breastfeeding, and in "Pretty Little Martha" he hopes vaguely that maybe he'll be reunited with her on her second birthday. But 1981's "Five Years Old" is still the birthday greeting of an absent father. Martha would comment later that he wrote songs about his children instead of raising them.

> Happy birthday Martha, happy birthday, birthday girl
> I'm sorry I can't be there for that party, birthday girl

Rufus and Martha were raised by their mother in Canada while their songwriting parents periodically traded blows in lyrics. For the children it must have been an awkwardly public commentary on their dysfunctional family. Loudon was often self-critical too, aware of his own shortcomings. "Hitting You" from the album *History*, his triumphant return to form in 1992, is a painfully confessional account of a car journey back from the beach, during which he lost his temper with Martha.

With both parents so articulate in expressing the family failings in music, it is hardly surprising that both children turned to song to express their own rage and hurt. As Martha recognizes now, "We just all have really big mouths—sometimes to our detriment."

Rufus described a bitter evening with his father in his song "Dinner at Eight," while Martha let it all hang out in her furious diatribe "Bloody Mother Fucking Asshole." Although she used to routinely introduce it as "a song about my dad," she now argues, "it can be about anybody and anything."

Prior to Kate's death in 2010, the family seemed to be coming, at least publicly, to some sort of understanding, ironically through the very medium of confessional songwriting which made Loudon Wainwright such an inattentive father. Looking back on her childhood, Martha joked, "It wasn't the Von Trapp family! But the issues I have with my mum and dad are much less than those most of my friends have with their parents probably— because there are no secrets."

Martha Wainwright, in turn, made her father the subject of one of her own songs.

LOUDON WAINWRIGHT III was one of many "new Dylans" who arose in the late 1960s—John Prine, David Blue, and others. He managed to carve a niche by infusing his songs with a trademark humor. Appearances as Captain Calvin Spalding (the "singing surgeon") on the TV show *M*A*S*H* presaged a later movie acting career. His role as father of musicians Rufus Wainwright, Martha Wainwright, and Lucy Wainwright Roche has now eclipsed his own musical achievements, but he remains well loved by a small and loyal following. In January 2010, Wainwright won a Grammy for Best Traditional Folk Album (*High Wide & Handsome*).

The Girl from Ipanema
Antônio Carlos Jobim / Vinicius de Moraes

Often heard as muzak in a public place or as a call-waiting tune, "The Girl from Ipanema" has ingrained itself into all walks of public life. But it was one girl's walk to the Brazilian beach every day that originally inspired the song.

Heloísa Eneida Menezes Paes Pinto was a fifteen-year-old living in Montenegro Street in Rio de Janeiro's upmarket Ipanema district. She would stroll past the popular café bar Veloso everyday and occasionally stop in to buy cigarettes for her mother. The Veloso was the meeting place for lyricist Vinicius de Moraes and musician Antônio Carlos Jobim, who felt compelled to describe the way she stole the attention of everyone she passed in a song they originally called "Menina que Passa" (The Girl Who Passes By).

> But each day when she walks to the sea
> She looks straight ahead not at me

Soon she would take notice, as the song would make her a celebrity. After the song was a massive worldwide hit for Astrud Gilberto, there was intense speculation as to who the girl from Ipanema was. Tired of the vast array of pretenders claiming to be "the girl," de Moraes held a press conference in 1965 and confirmed the girl was Heloísa. He said rather poetically, "She is a golden girl, a mixture of flowers and mermaids, full of light and full of grace, but whose character is also sad with the feeling that youth passes and that beauty isn't ours to keep. She is the gift of life with its beautiful and melancholic constant ebb and flow." Heloísa received public recognition but unsurprisingly did not make any money from the track directly.

The song won a Grammy for Record of the Year in 1965, throwing it, and its inspiration, even more firmly into the limelight. Her fame kept her in the public eye (in Brazil at least), and a 1987 *Playboy* pictorial (at age forty) and a subsequent appearance with her daughter in 2003 showed that time had been kind to the woman from Ipanema. But controversy abounded when Heloísa (now Pinheiro after her marriage to Fernando, a

Heloísa is still a celebrity in Brazil with her own chain of clothes shops.

Sao Paolo engineer) decided to open a boutique under the song title's Portuguese translation, Garota de Ipanema.

De Moraes and Jobim's children attempted to sue her for cashing in on their fathers' song. The judge in the case disagreed and ruled in favor of Pinheiro, who had commented on her sadness before the case, "[Jobim] used to say to me that 'The Girl from Ipanema' was the goose that laid the golden egg, but I never made a cent from any of that, nor do I claim that I should. Yet now that I'm using a legally registered trademark, they want to prohibit me from being the girl from Ipanema, which is really going too far."

Famed for her daily walk to worship the sun, Pinheiro became the mythical object of many a man's desire. But for the descendants of the song's creators, the desire was, it seemed, purely pecuniary.

ANTÔNIO CARLOS JOBIM's composition "The Girl from Ipanema" brought Brazilian music to a worldwide audience back in 1964. Joao Gilberto from Brazil allied to the talents of U.S. jazz saxman Stan Getz. Gilberto, from Bahia in northern Brazil, was first to record "Ipanema," singing in Portuguese, but when his wife Astrud took it to #5 in the American charts in 1964, it was sung in English, the vocalist joined by Getz and Jobim. The song had been written in 1962, with music by Antônio Carlos Jobim and Portuguese lyrics by Vinícius de Moraes, English lyrics were written later by Norman Gimbel. While "Ipanema" would remain his greatest hit, Jobim continued as an influential performer and songwriter, collaborating with many Brazilian and foreign writers. His genius was confirmed when Frank Sinatra and Ella Fitzgerald both separately recorded albums of his songs. After his death in 1994, Rio's airport was named after him.

Hearts and Bones
Paul Simon

By the time the album *Hearts and Bones* was released in 1983, Paul Simon's solo career had lost all momentum. He was never prolific. It was three years since his previous effort, *One Trick Pony*, and that had appeared five long years after its 1975 predecessor, *Still Crazy After All These Years*. In the early 1980s he had been distracted by a prolonged but unsatisfactory reunion with Art Garfunkel, a retrograde step which resulted in a crippling bout of writer's block. He was also wrestling during that period with a tempestuous relationship with actress Carrie Fisher.

> You take two bodies and you twirl them into one
> Their hearts and their bones
> And they won't come undone

Simon and Fisher had met in 1978. Although it is very clear that they loved each other deeply (and still hold each other in high affection), it was a troubled affair, full of fights and separations. They were poorly matched—she a West Coast daughter of hedonistic Hollywood, he an East Coast son of neurotic New York. Their short-lived marriage in 1983 was an ill-conceived last-ditch attempt to save the relationship. It collapsed finally under the strain of Fisher's battle with substance abuse, which itself was a symptom of her undiagnosed bipolar disorder.

Commentators note wryly that the breakup with Carrie Fisher was Paul Simon's third and most traumatic divorce, following those from his first wife, Peggy Harper, and his singing partner, Art Garfunkel. Simon, the literate and confessional composer, has reflected on all three in song—notably about Garfunkel in "So Long Frank Lloyd Wright" and Harper in "Train in the Distance." "Hearts and Bones," now regarded by many as his finest love song, is about his time with Carrie, "the arc of a love affair waiting to be restored."

His divorce from Fisher, after six years together but only eleven months of marriage, coincided with relatively poor sales for the album. *Hearts and Bones* has since been reevaluated as one of his best collections. But at the time he had lost the public's attention, and his exploration of a

With Carrie Fisher in 1983, the year they married. They divorced eleven months later.

new lyrical mixture of casual conversation and more poetic language was not universally well received.

At a very low ebb and feeling that he had nothing to lose, he struck out in a new direction after listening to a tape of South African township music in his car. The resulting album, *Graceland*, fused this sound with the lyrical style of *Hearts and Bones* and was a triumphant return to popularity. The title track of the new album was a further meditation on the aftermath of his time with Carrie.

Carrie Fisher has survived drugs and depression to become a successful author. She has published fictionalized accounts of her dependencies (*Postcards from the Edge*) and her relationship with Paul (*Surrender the Pink*), while an autobiography, *Wishful Drinking*, has now become a successful one-woman stage show. In the show she admits to finding it "trippy" to hear songs on the radio about a relationship that ended over twenty-five years ago. Nevertheless, she tells her audience, "If you can get Paul Simon to write a song for you … DO IT!"

PAUL SIMON is perhaps better known for his career with Art Garfunkel. But Simon went it alone in 1970, going on to enjoy further success in his own right. *Hearts and Bones* was the title track of Simon's fifth album, but it was only released in single format as the B-side to "Graceland" in 1986.

Graceland, the peak of Simon's solo success, sold more than fourteen million copies and won the Album of the Year Grammy Award. Several onstage reunions with Garfunkel followed, and Simon continues to release solo LPs and tour; however new Simon & Garfunkel recordings are an unlikely prospect.

Hey Negrita
The Rolling Stones

The recording of the album *Black and Blue* took place in six sessions over a period of fourteen months. It served as a rolling audition in the Rolling Stones' search for a replacement for Mick Taylor, who had quit the band in December 1974. A spectacular array of guest musicians contributed to tracks along the way, just to see how they would gel with Jagger, Richards, Wyman, and Watts.

Some unlikely names were up for the job: Peter Frampton, Rory Gallagher, and Jeff Beck, all with strong solo careers underway, seem in retrospect unsuitable candidates to play second fiddle to Keith Richards. In the end, of course, it was Ronnie Wood of the Faces who got the gig. He remembers his first recording session with the band in March 1975: "I had this particular lick that I took into the studio, and the others said, 'What are we going to start with?' I said, 'I've got this song.' Charlie was sitting behind his kit, so he was already into it and then Keith and Mick both got into the motion of it. That was 'Hey Negrita,' which came together very easily."

It was 1975. Bob Marley was the big new sound and for a while (so it seemed) every white rock band in the land felt obliged to include their idea of a reggae-flavored track on their next album. Ronnie Wood's riff was just that; but married with Richards's trademark R & B vamp and Watt's rocksteady beat, "Hey Negrita" was a more successful fusion than some.

> Hey Negrita, hey now
> Move your body, move your mouth
> Shake lady, way down south

Mick improvised the lyrics. Negrita was his nickname for Bianca Jagger, his wife at the time. She was Nicaraguan, and the word means "little black girl" in Spanish. The rest of the lyrics tell the story of a poor South American man getting short shrift when he tries to buy a prostitute on the cheap. In the changing social politics of 1976, when *Black and Blue* was finally released, this sort of thing was bound to get the Stones into trouble.

There was a torrent of criticism about the song and about the billboard advertisements for the album, which showed a bruised and provocatively bound woman declaring, "I'm Black and Blue from the Rolling Stones—and I love it!" The band was seen as racist and sexist, the poster boys of outdated dinosaur rock which punk and New Wave became dedicated to eradicating. There is, however, no such thing as bad publicity, and the howls of protest probably only helped cement the Stones' position as perpetual bad boys, the original rebels, and the franchise holders of the Greatest Rock and Roll Band in the World.

Jagger was of course dismissive of the objections, defending at least the title of the song as a typically South American term of affection. In any case, white reggae had a pretty short shelf life, and the song was never played live again after the band's European tour of 1976. Its final

Marital bliss. Bianca Jagger later commented, "My marriage ended on my wedding day."

performance was at the massive Knebworth Fayre festival on August 21, at which Jagger strutted his stuff on a long, forward-jutting tongue-shaped walkway. The whole stage was framed by a huge inflatable (one might almost say "overblown") pair of Rolling Stones lips.

And what of Bianca? She seems to have survived marriage to the Rolling Stones better than many. The woman to whom Jagger addressed this affectionate lyric had married him in 1971, although she later declared, "My marriage ended on my wedding day." When Mick seduced Brian Ferry's fiancée, Jerry Hall, in 1977 and began a long affair with her, Bianca left him and filed for divorce, which was finalized two years later.

She had already begun to immerse herself in high-profile human rights campaigning, taking full advantage of her married name to attract attention to many important causes. After her divorce (she retained her ex-husband's surname), she publicized the brutality of the Somoza regime in her home country and fought against U.S. intervention when that regime was overthrown by the Sandinistas. She has spoken out in favor of indigenous peoples elsewhere in South America, notably those whose traditional ways of life are under threat from development in the Amazon basin.

In recent years she has argued for the closure of the U.S. detention center at Guantanamo Bay and for the prosecution of war criminals in the former Yugoslavia. She is a goodwill ambassador for the Council of Europe, speaking on its behalf against the death penalty.

THE ROLLING STONES included "Hey Negrita" on their album *Black and Blue*, which was also their first with new guitarist Ronnie Wood. "Fool to Cry" was the most successful song from the LP, reaching #6 and #10 in the U.K. and U.S. respectively. The album was released in 1976 during an incredible run of eight consecutive U.S. #1 albums for the Stones, starting with *Sticky Fingers* in 1971 and ending with *Tattoo You* a decade later. The band's follow-up album, *Some Girls*, released in 1978, would perform even better, going platinum six times in the U.S.

Bianca and Mick in 1973, when they were the ultimate jet-setting, party-going couple.

Bianca Jagger's early successes in putting rights abuses into the spotlight were certainly helped by her celebrity marriage. But it has been more than thirty years since she became very much her own woman. Her contribution to human rights since her divorce is enormous, not merely the work of a rock star's ex-wife but the achievements of a genuinely committed and recognized campaigner. She has been the recipient of awards from everyone from Mikhail Gorbachev to the United Nations. It must therefore be very frustrating to see herself still, three decades later, almost universally referred to as "Bianca Jagger, ex-wife of Rolling Stones frontman Mick Jagger." As she says, "I find it disturbing that the media keeps referring to my marriage, since I got divorced in 1979. But the media never wants to let me forget."

Spare a thought for Ronnie Wood, whose riff was the source and the rhythm of "Hey Negrita." Mick Jagger and Keith Richards have kept a tight rein on the writing credits for all Rolling Stones material since the early 1970s. So it is with "Hey Negrita"—the composers are listed, as always, as Jagger, Richards. An afterthought in the sleeve notes of *Black and Blue* reads: "Inspiration by Ronnie Wood."

In the Air Tonight
Phil Collins

Phil Collins's career in showbiz began not as a singer on huge hits like "In the Air Tonight," nor even as a drummer with prog-rock giants Genesis. His first steps were as a child actor. His mother was London casting agent June Collins, and in 1964 he made his movie debut as an extra in the Beatles film *A Hard Day's Night*. In the same year he enjoyed a seven-month run as the Artful Dodger in the West End musical *Oliver!* When his voice broke, he had to leave the production, and he enrolled at stage school. It was there that he first met fellow students Lavinia Lang and Andrea Bertorelli.

Phil dated both girls over the next few years. Lavinia had also worked as an extra in the Beatles film and later became a member of leather-clad dance group Hot Gossip.

It was after Lavinia and Phil split in 1969 that he started going out with Andrea. When that fizzled out, Andrea returned to her native Vancouver. Fast forward to 1974, when Andrea and Phil met up again after a Genesis show in the city, picking up more or less where they left off. The following year she flew back to England and the couple married. Collins went so far as to adopt Joely, Andrea's daughter from a failed earlier relationship in Vancouver.

Collins also took over the lead vocal role in Genesis that year and steered the already successful rock band towards global and lucrative pop-chart success. In 1976 the couple had a second child, Simon.

In 1978 Genesis were touring constantly, ironically to promote their new album, *And Then There Were Three*. Phil's frequent absences on tour strained the family to breaking point. Isolated at home, lonely Andrea had an affair with a painter-decorator. When Phil found out, the marriage fell apart, and in 1979 Andrea returned to Vancouver with their children. It was one evening in the aftermath of their departure, when Phil had finished another long Genesis tour and returned to his empty family home, that he sought comfort in his home recording studio.

He sat down, turned on his tape deck and his drum machine, and improvised a few sad piano chords. Then he got up to sing, and all the pain and anger flooded out. "The lyrics you hear for 'In the Air Tonight,' I just sang," he said later. "I opened my mouth and they came out. I never wrote anything down." He performed the song on the BBC with a paint pot and brushes balanced on the top of his piano, a wry nod to his ex-wife's lover.

Other songs from the album also dealt with the breakup of his family, including the next two singles, "I Missed Again" and "If Leaving Me Is Easy." Speaking after the release of *Face Value*, Collins protested, "I had a wife, two children, two dogs, and the next day I didn't have anything." The follow-up album, *Hello, I Must Be Going!* continued the theme of bitterness, loss, and injury.

Joely, Phil, and Andrea in 1976, the year Collins stepped into Peter Gabriel's shoes as Genesis vocalist.

Andrea still lives in Vancouver, where, according to her daughter's Web site, she is an environmental activist. Simon Collins, Andrea and Phil's son, is a Germany-based musician with three successful solo albums to his credit.

Joely Collins followed in her parents' theatrical footsteps. After training at Vancouver Youth Theatre and London's Royal Academy of Dramatic Art, she made her acting debut as Rachel Langston in the TV series *Madison* in 1993. The role won her a Canadian TV award, the Gemini, for Best Leading Actress. In 2008 she made Phil Collins a granddad.

PHIL COLLINS made his name with British rock band Genesis before embarking on a solo career that would see him sell more than 150 million records. In a career spanning over forty years, Collins starred in the film *Buster* and even won an Oscar, though it was for penning a track to Disney's 1999 animated feature *Tarzan*. In the 1990s he racked up seven U.S. #1 singles. Genesis reformed for a tour in 2008. A neck injury has forced him to stop playing the drums and piano, though he continues to sing.

Irene Wilde
Ian Hunter

Ian Hunter Patterson took a long time to get his rock 'n' roll career off the ground. Born in rural Shropshire, he played in small local bands and aspirant London bands throughout the late 1950s and 1960s. He eventually joined up with Hereford band Shakedown Sound who, according to their manager Guy Stevens, needed a frontman with some charisma. Together they became known as Mott the Hoople. Despite critical acclaim their record sales were disappointing; they were on the brink of splitting up when David Bowie, a big fan of the band, gave them "Suffragette City" as a single. They turned it down, so he gave them "All the Young Dudes" instead, and it became a major hit.

Barker Street bus station in Shrewsbury where Ian Patterson stood "waiting for a dream," Irene Wilde.

Hunter left the band in 1975 to go solo and headed for the States, where in 1976 he released his second solo album, *All-American Alien Boy*. The album contained one of the most poignant songs about teenage love and rejection, "Irene Wilde."

The story charts how Ian waited at a bus station for a girl who just looked at him with scorn.

> For those looks they seemed to say
> You ain't nuthin'—go away
> You're just a face in the crowd, so I went home and I vowed
> I'm gonna be somebody—someday

The song was also included on the successful 1980 live double album, *Welcome to the Club*, where Hunter introduces the song with the line. "People ask me if this is a true story," and the audience responds in unison, "Ian, is this a true story?" It is. In the song Hunter tells how, after seeing some fame, he returns to "that country town" to play a gig and sees her face in the crowd. Only now he's too proud to talk to her.

There has been no postsong meeting, though. "She knows about the song, somebody told me," he wrote on his Web site. "There was always this guy, Brian Poole, hanging about, and every time I went with these girls—if I left town or something like that—he would immediately step in. I remember he had this crimson velvet jacket and I always envied that jacket. And he wound up with Irene Wilde. He married her, and they had twins. But that last time I saw her, she didn't look at all like the girl I remembered."

IAN HUNTER did all manner of jobs before taking on the role of frontman of Mott the Hoople at age 30. The band morphed from a close-to-splitting progressive rock band into a successful glam-rock outfit, thanks to the last minute intervention of David Bowie. Hunter chronicled the band's five-week American tour of 1972 in *Diary of a Rock 'n' Roll Star*, considered one of the finest self-penned rock journals. In 1975 Hunter went solo with the eponymous *Ian Hunter* album, which included barnstorming single "Once Bitten Twice Shy." Marrying an American and basing himself Stateside, Hunter maintained a cult singer-songwriter career through the first decade of the twenty-first century, often collaborating with former Spiders from Mars guitarist Mick Ronson. Hunter celebrated his seventieth year with a multidate Mott the Hoople reunion in 2009 at the Hammersmith Apollo (previously the Odeon), the scene of so much British rock history and the last-known resting place of Ziggy Stardust.

It Ain't Me Babe
Bob Dylan

Bob Dylan is one of the most important figures in modern music. His thirty-four studio albums span five decades, and his impact on folk and rock music have made him a genuine legend.

But when Joan Baez met the up-and-coming young troubadour in 1961 in New York's bohemian Greenwich Village, she was the more famous of the pair. Yet Baez immediately saw potential in the man from Minnesota. She recalls their first meeting: "I'd been told that I absolutely had to hear this guy. He was just fantastic and that's all I'd heard. So I was prepared to see somebody who wasn't going to live up to everything I'd heard. And that's not what I saw. He was clearly a jewel of some kind."

Baez herself was already an established musician, having emerged with her self-titled debut album a year earlier. *Joan Baez* was an independently released collection of folk songs that had brought her to public attention.

Her second LP was released at the end of 1961, reaching #13 on the Billboard 200 and receiving a Grammy nomination for Best Contemporary Folk Performance. Baez was hot property, and her friendship with Dylan gathered increasing media attention.

Baez was impressed with Dylan's passion for social change, which she shared, and was particularly enamored with his early songs. "It was as if he was giving voice to the ideas I wanted to express, but didn't know how."

So much did she believe in his work and his message that she introduced him to the public by bringing him onstage at her shows. Soon Dylan himself would turn heads, and he signed with major label Columbia. His eponymous debut LP was released in 1962, reaching #13 in the U.K.

Baez began incorporating a number of Dylan tracks into her repertoire; "Don't Think Twice, It's All Right" featured on her 1963 album *Joan Baez in Concert, Part 2*, while 1965's *Farewell Angelina* LP featured no less than four songs written by him.

Although she was a talented songwriter, it would be Baez's penchant for playing other artists' material that would ultimately hold her back.

Baez and Dylan performing together at a civil rights rally in Washington, D.C., August 28, 1963, where Martin Luther King delivered his "I Have a Dream" speech.

Dylan's career would skyrocket as his songwriting matured. His second album, *The Freewheelin' Bob Dylan*, reached #1 in the U.K. and charted just outside the U.S. Top 20. The lady on the cover was Dylan's on-off girlfriend, artist Suze Rotolo, who was the casualty in Baez and Dylan's blossoming relationship.

Rotolo said of it later, "It's a very long time ago, and there are no residual hurt feelings. I think [Baez is] an example of a woman who really knew what she wanted and how to get it, and to everybody else, the hell with you."

Baez and Dylan's passion for change was what attracted them and held them together early in their relationship. In 1963 they were both involved in the famous March on Washington, during which Martin Luther King delivered his "I Have a Dream" speech. They both played at the event, with Baez singing the anthemic "We Shall Overcome" to the estimated 250,000 in attendance.

In May 1963, Dylan had performed with Baez at the Monterey Folk Festival, where she joined him on stage to duet on a new Dylan song, "With God on Our Side." Baez was at the pinnacle of her fame, having appeared on the cover of *Time* magazine the previous November.

Meanwhile, Dylan wanted to distance himself from becoming "the voice of protest" and was gradually moving toward other styles of music and different messages. The consequence was the breakdown of his brief relationship with Baez.

In later years Baez looked back on her romance with the folk icon and the pressure of a relationship under public scrutiny. "Dylan and I were not just two people—we were thousands of people, everybody else's images of whatever we were, none of them true. But why it was so huge I don't really know."

Sticking to her principles, Baez continued to wage her wars on several fronts. She protested against the U.S. involvement in Vietnam, withholding taxes and returning to Washington to protest.

Her work for racial equality continued into 1966, assisting Martin Luther King Jr. on rallies in the South and participated in further antiwar rallies. She found herself behind bars on two occasions in 1967 for protests against the Vietnam War.

She married journalist and fellow protester David Harris in 1968 after a whirlwind romance, the pair having met when Baez was incarcerated the previous year. But Dylan's imprint on her life was still evident professionally if not personally; she released *Any Day Now*, a double-CD collection of Dylan tracks the same year, which went gold.

Baez had a child with Harris in 1969. Son Gabriel was not enough to keep the pair together, however, and they separated in 1973. Two years later she released *Diamonds and Rust*, an LP regarded by critics and fans alike as Baez's finest work. It included self-penned songs, most notably the title track that was about Dylan.

At the same time she was reunited with Dylan, touring with his Rolling Thunder Revue. He had gone on to marry Sarah Lownds in November 1965, with whom he had a son, Jakob, in 1969; the marriage would last until June 1977.

Throughout the 1980s and 1990s Baez continued to protest for civil rights, equality, and nonviolence, and was involved in 1985's Live Aid concerts. In 2007 she finally picked up a Grammy after missing out through her career, despite six nominations.

Though eventually left in the shadows of her one-time protégé and lover, Joan Baez

Sharing a stage together at the Newport Festival, Rhode Island, July 1963.

enjoyed a hugely successful career lasting more than fifty years, which spanned not just music but many other issues in life about which she felt strongly. No wonder Bob Dylan was so enamored with the singer from Staten Island, New York. But ultimately, as she looked for a partner to help her change the world, he told her, "It ain't me, babe."

BOB DYLAN released "It Ain't Me Babe" on his fourth album, 1964's *Another Side of Bob Dylan.* He was about to take his controversial step into electrified rock, and when he played his first "plugged" concerts in 1965 he gave the song an electric arrangement. Dylan and Johnny Cash admired each other's work and, with Dylan's blessing, Cash recorded the song with wife June Carter and included it on his 1965 album, *Orange Blossom Special.* Since Dylan didn't release it as a single, harmony pop band the Turtles filled the gap with a cover and had a hit with the song. When Dylan's record

company Columbia released his first greatest-hits compilation in 1967, "It Ain't Me Babe" took its rightful place, as it was one of just three tracks that had not been issued on seven-inch plastic.

It Ain't Over 'til It's Over
Lenny Kravitz

Lenny Kravitz announced his arrival on the music scene in 1988 at twenty-four, under the alias Romeo Blue, he had already met his muse, actress Lisa Bonet, who would prove to be the inspiration of one of his biggest hits, as well as his future wife.

After reverting back to his given name, Kravitz released debut album *Let Love Rule* in 1989. The LP, on which he played a variety of instruments, sold two million copies worldwide and displayed his diversity, as it featured elements of rock, funk, and soul. It also featured songwriting credits on two tracks for Bonet.

Bonet herself was hot property, appearing in popular sitcom *The Cosby Show*, which began in 1984. The pair had eloped on her twentieth birthday in 1987, when Kravitz was a relative unknown, causing a tabloid stir. Kravitz credited Bonet for inspiring his debut. "We both just had something that was incredibly magic. So when I started hanging out with her is when I started writing *Let Love Rule*."

Happier times: Kravitz and Bonet on the town in 1989.

Her take: "It was interesting when we were first finding out about each other, that our backgrounds were so similar. When I first told him my mom was Jewish, and he said 'So's my dad,' I thought that was both unusual and enchanting. I felt like, 'Okay, here's someone who really knows how it is.' And I think I trusted him a little more with my feelings and let him inside a little more than I ordinarily would have."

The birth of their daughter, Zoe, in 1988 looked to cement the couple's fairytale-like romance, but it would prove to be their last happy moment before it all began to unravel.

Kravitz had begun collaborating with pop diva Madonna, penning her #1 track "Justify My Love," and the same media that lapped up his marriage to Bonet took equal pleasure in having a hand in its downfall. Reports of romantic involvement with Madonna and others caused the married couple to separate in 1991, sparking yet more creative inspiration for Kravitz when he began penning tracks for his second album, *Mama Said*. "That album was a big haze, because Lisa and I had split and it was a very heavy time. That whole second album was about her, dedicated to her."

"It Ain't Over 'til It's Over" was Kravitz's apology to Bonet for his indiscretions and a plea for another try with the actress and mother of his child. "I was trying to redirect myself and say 'Hey, I blew it, but I'm going to get it right.' At that point it was kind of too late, I suppose."

Kravitz would later reconnect with Bonet while recording his fifth studio album; her positive influence on the singer was again evident as the album, *5*, picked up two consecutive Male Rock Vocal Grammy awards in 1999 and 2000 for "Fly Away" and "American Woman."

He and Bonet divorced in 1993; by then she had legally changed her name to Lilakoi Moon, though she still uses the name Lisa Bonet for her entertainment career. She continues to act, and has had two further children with Jason Momoa, an actor noted for roles in television shows *Baywatch* and *Stargate Atlantis*. Ironically he boasts dreadlocks similar to Kravitz's, though the singer has since shorn his early hairstyle. Their daughter has a burgeoning acting career.

Producer and singer-songwriter LENNY KRAVITZ has brought his funk rock and R & B to the masses since 1989. His debut LP, *Let Love Rule*, sold more than two million copies. Since then he has released eight studio albums and received multiple awards, the highlight of which was winning the Best Male Rock Vocal Performance Grammy for four consecutive years (1999–2003).

Kravitz released "It Ain't Over 'til It's Over" in 1991, and it reached #2 in the U.S. and #11 in the U.K.

His other single successes include "Are You Gonna Go My Way," "Again," and "Fly Away."

Je T'Aime (Moi Non Plus)

Jane Birkin and Serge Gainsbourg

The 1960s was, to many, a shocking decade, but Serge Gainsbourg's "Je T'Aime (Moi Non Plus)," with its repeatedly whispered title plus simulated lovemaking noises atop an organ backing, pushed the boundaries as far as any other musical statement. It was inspired by one woman, actress-model-singer Brigitte Bardot, and performed most famously with English actress-singer Jane Birkin.

Bardot had already recorded a few Gainsbourg songs before they appeared together on a prime-time TV show in late 1967. Bardot's second marriage was in trouble, and she and Gainsbourg discovered a mutual attraction. She invited him to appear on her own TV show, and he began writing new songs for her. They had acted together in French films as early as 1959, but now they were also lovers.

They sang Gainsbourg's songs on her show. The set for "Comic Strip" reflected the pop psychedelia of the time; while performing "Bonnie and Clyde," they styled themselves as crooks.

Bardot had asked Gainsbourg to write her "the most beautiful love song you can think of," and he recorded a song that was musically inspired by the previous year's megahit, "A Whiter Shade of Pale," in 1968. But when gossip emanated about supposed heavy petting at the sessions, her husband, German industrialist Gunther Sachs, demanded the release be withdrawn.

Jane Birkin was happy to take her place. Birkin had followed in the footsteps of her mother, Judy Gamble, who in her time was a renowned actress and a muse of playwright Noel Coward. She grew up in an artistic environment with elder brother Andrew and sister Linda.

In 1968 French director Pierre Grimblat began looking for a young English actress to star in his film *Slogan*. Birkin ventured across the Channel to audition for the female lead, never suspecting she was leaving England behind for good. Grimblat had originally intended to cast Marisa Berenson but was so impressed by Jane's audition that he offered her the part, even though at that time she did not speak a word of French.

She and Gainsbourg, who had recently turned forty, met and fell in love on the set of *Slogan*. She was at that time the estranged wife of celebrated film composer John Barry (by whom she had a daughter) and was best known for revealing all while romping with actor David Hemmings in the Antonioni film *Blow-Up* (1966).

"Serge made up this love song that means 'I love you, nor do I'," she explained. "He asked me to sing it an octave higher than Bardot so I would sound like a choirboy. I said yes because I was far too afraid that some other beautiful girl would sing it in my place."

Another female, Queen Juliana of the Netherlands, did intervene, using her position as major shareholder in Philips Records to have the song withdrawn. By this time it had reached #2 in Britain

September 1959: poet, actor, singer, and writer Serge Gainsbourg stands by as Brigitte Bardot waltzes past. They were on the set of French movie Come Dance with Me, *directed by Michel Boisrond.*

on Philips's Fontana label. It was banned by the BBC (which instead played an instrumental cover version called "Love at First Sight") and denounced by the Vatican in a statement in official newspaper *L'Osservatore*. But the genuine "Je T'Aime" swiftly resurfaced on Irish independent label Major Minor and became a Europe-wide hit, with sales topping the million mark in France alone. Gainsbourg declared it the "ultimate love song."

The lyrics depict an imaginary dialogue in French between two lovers during a sexual encounter. Phrases from the song—prior to its culmination in a simulated orgasm from Birkin—include:

Je T'Aime (Moi Non Plus) | **53**

Je vais et je viens, entre tes reins ("I go and I come,
in between your loins")

Tu es la vague, moi l'île nue ("You are the wave,
I the naked island")

L'amour physique est sans issue ("Physical love has
no strings attached")

Birkin has since revealed the song was recorded in a studio near London's Marble Arch and that, during the take, her partner kept making sign language "to calm down the huffing and puffing. He was frightened I wasn't going to make the highest note."

Jane moved into Gainsbourg's Paris apartment in the rue de Verneuil, and the couple settled down to a calmer existence. Kate, Jane's daughter from her first marriage, began to spend more time with them, and Gainsbourg would bring her up as his own.

Gainsbourg and Birkin together in Paris in 1969, around the time of the single's release. He was 40, she was 23.

On a professional level, the incorrigible Gainsbourg continued to push the boundaries of acceptability, moving into film direction in 1975 when he directed Birkin in a film named after their hit. In it she played a boy and became the love interest of a gay trucker.

Gainsbourg and Birkin never married but enjoyed a lengthy relationship, which produced a daughter, actress and singer Charlotte Gainsbourg. They separated in 1980; two years later Birkin gave birth to her third daughter, Lou Doillon, from her relationship with the director Jacques Doillon.

She continued to act and sing, and the creative collaboration with Gainsbourg paradoxically flourished once reestablished in 1983. "You would think it would have been more difficult to work together after we split up but it was quite the opposite. When we were together he always wrote me rather light songs. I would be a sweet Lolita character, sometimes a little like a prostitute or a naughty hitchhiker picking up lorry drivers." Afterwards, she explained, the songs became darker and had more depth. The release of the album *Version Jane* in 1995, entirely made up of Gainsbourg classics, included a roll call of modern French musicians whom Birkin had invited to help her rearrange the songs.

Jane has also had a fashionable handbag—the Birkin bag—named after her in 1984 by Hermès. She has become involved in humanitarian causes connected with immigrant welfare and AIDS, and has been awarded the British OBE and the French Ordre National du Mérite in recognition of those efforts.

Gainsbourg died in 1991 and, while Birkin has continued to sing his songs in concert, she has never to date performed "Je T'Aime (Moi Non Plus)." Yet she is still proud of her greatest hit. "I was told by a taxi driver during a recent visit to London that he'd had three children on that record. So pourquoi pas? If you're going to be famous for just one thing, it's a pretty nice thing to be famous for." The original Brigitte Bardot version was finally released on a compilation LP in the mid-1980s.

SERGE GAINSBOURG (1928–1991) may have been known outside France primarily for the heavy-breathing masterpiece "Je T'Aime (Moi Non Plus)," the only French song ever to top the British charts; but to those at home he stood as one of the more potent cultural figures of postwar France. His poetry was compared to Rimbaud and Baudelaire, his morality to the Marquis de Sade, and his sobriety to Thénadier in *Les Miserables*. He was awarded the Chevalier Des Arts et Lettres, his country's highest artistic honor. Joann Sfar's film biography, *Serge Gainsbourg—Vie Héroique* was released in 2010 and starred Eric Elmosnino as the man himself.

JANE BIRKIN has been a superstar in France for four decades. Her status as popular icon is due not only to the many movies in which she has appeared but also to her relationship with Serge Gainsbourg and the music they made together.

Jennifer Juniper
Donovan

Although Jenny Boyd married two rock musicians, it was Scottish troubadour Donovan who famously composed a musical tribute to her. Willowy blonde Jenny followed in older sister Pattie's footsteps as a fashion model. Pattie married George Harrison, which brought Jenny into the Beatles' inner circle. Jenny started to work in the group's short-lived Apple Boutique and traveled to the ashram in India to learn Transcendental Meditation with them.

In autumn 1967, she posed with Donovan, another Beatle confidante, at Bodiam Castle in East Sussex for the photoshoot for the cover of his album, *A Gift from a Flower to a Garden*. Entranced by Jenny's charms, he wrote "Jennifer Juniper" for her. "I had a crush on Jenny so she got a song," Donovan explained. He denies rumors that he and Jenny had an affair, even though they took a trip to Greece together.

Released as a single early in 1968, the song's lyric, with the final verse in French, was framed in question-and-response style. That year, the Boyd sisters opened an antique stall in the King's Road Market, Chelsea, calling it Juniper in acknowledgment of the song. "Juniper" is a variation of "Jennifer"; both names share the same source. Interestingly, her real name is Helen Mary Boyd; "Jenny" was a nickname coined by Pattie, after a favorite doll.

No stranger to the hedonistic side of 1960s culture, Jenny's experiments with marijuana and LSD landed her in court in 1968. She was charged with possession. Her drug use also led to a revelation: "One momentous day I experienced an astonishing realization, which I can now identify as a spiritual awakening. The traditional Christian beliefs I had been taught as a child crumbled as I suddenly recognized that there was no God above or hell below. God was everywhere, inside each one of us. I saw everything as a circle: life, death, and rebirth, or reincarnation."

At the time, she was involved in a stormy, on-off relationship with Fleetwood Mac drummer Mick Fleetwood, who had fallen under her spell when she was just 15. Jenny recalled that, in 1966, "I met someone in Rome and became involved. I told Mick when I got home and he got really upset. It was a very big break-up."

They eventually reconciled, marrying in June 1970. When they relocated to Los Angeles in 1974 she began to further explore her spiritual side. The recruitment of Lindsey Buckingham and Stevie Nicks began a remarkable upturn in Fleetwood Mac's fortunes, but it hastened the end of Jenny and Mick's marriage. She fled back to England for a few months, returning to L.A. to remarry Mick in 1976. But the phenomenal success of the band's *Rumours* album and the couple's increasing use of drug and alcohol precipitated the final end of their fifteen-year relationship only six months later.

For a time Jenny Boyd worked at The Beatles' ill-fated Apple Boutique.

Jenny married former King Crimson drummer Ian Wallace In 1984, and the couple divided their time between California and Surrey before Wallace's death in 2007. Pursuing her interest in psychology, Jenny took a degree in humanities, a master's degree in counseling psychology, and finally a PhD in 1989 after which she became a clinical consultant. She combined the recurring themes of her life by writing *Musicians in Tune,* a book about musicians and the psychology of creativity.

DONOVAN Leitch was discovered while busking on the streets before signing a recording contract. He came to prominence in the folk boom of the 1960s, aligning himself first with Bob Dylan and then the Beatles. The hippie singer-songwriter gained success in both the U.K. and America, scoring #1 singles and albums. He was one of the many who attended the ashram in India along with the Beatles and Jenny Boyd. "Jennifer Juniper" was released in 1968 after Donovan had already gained fame in the U.S. with his song "Sunshine Superman"; he enjoyed similar success in his home country with his take on fellow folksinger Buffy Sainte-Marie's "Universal Soldier." He gathered more Top 40 albums throughout the 1970s before his popularity and relevance waned. He is the father of actress Ione Skye Leitch.

Life on Mars?

David Bowie

> It's a god-awful small affair
> To the girl with the mousy hair

The lyrics to "Life on Mars?" are usually categorized as baffling and obscure, but they are really just a collection of images of alienation and confusion. Taken overall, they create a remarkably clear impression of Bowie's intended meaning—the sense of being adrift in a modern, media-saturated world. "The girl with the mousy hair," is a reference to Hermione Farthingale, whom Bowie had met at a Lindsay Kemp mime workshop. Hermione came from an affluent home and was the archetypal English rose: attractive, willowy, and self-possessed. She and David quickly became lovers and later worked together, along with Lindsay Kemp, on the set of a 1968 TV drama, *The Pistol Shot*, from the BBC2 series *Theatre 625*. Kemp, who had become another of David's bed partners at this time, recalls being insanely jealous of Hermione: "I can remember the agony of the journey back from Television Centre when he was tagging along with her. I was livid."

Farthingale (whose real name has never been disclosed) was an habitué of the London folk scene and an aspiring ballet dancer, singer, and actress. She became Bowie's first serious girlfriend, and in August 1968 they moved into a rented room at 22 Clareville Grove in South Kensington. In September of the same year they formed an experimental folk trio with Tony Hill. Hill was quickly replaced by John Hutchinson, former guitarist for David Bowie and the Buzz. Originally called Turquoise, they were soon rechristened Feathers. Hutchinson, like David, was from a working-class background and was slightly in awe of Hermione, remembering her as being "a nice lass, but a bit posh.... I was always very careful not to swear in front of her." Feathers' mixed-media performances, which incorporated singing, dancing, poetry, and mime, mainly played to university halls and folk clubs and were greeted with a limited degree of success. Bowie would later dismiss his work with Feathers as an excuse to spend more time with Hermione.

Early in 1969 Bowie made an avant-garde film called *Love You Till Tuesday* to showcase nine of his songs, including a hastily written late

Bowie at the center of "performance" trio Feathers, with Hermione Furthingale and Tony Hill. Marc Bolan booked them as a tour support, thinking they were a mime act.

addition, "Space Oddity." He cast Hermione in the film sequence for that song as a seductive space maiden. But on the last day of her shoot, the day before he went into the studio to record the song, the pair had a blazing row. She had begun a relationship with Stephen Reinhardt, a Norwegian dancer and musician, and after the argument she walked out on Bowie.

Some of David's friends speculated that Hermione's middle-class parents disapproved of their relationship, while others felt that Hermione herself might not have been too pleased to learn that David also slept with men. In a press release later that year Bowie succinctly summarized his affair with Hermione, noting that he'd fallen in love at "twenty-one and three quarters" and was "solo again" at twenty-two. But as one love affair ended another was about to begin. It was while performing at the Roundhouse in January 1969, where Feathers was one of the acts supporting the Who, that Bowie was briefly introduced to his future wife, Angela.

Farthingale, who was indeed "hooked to the silver screen," went on to forge a short career in musical film; that year she appeared in *Oh! What a Lovely War* (as a chorus girl) and the Grieg biopic *Song of Norway* (as a dancer). Stephen Reinhardt also worked on the latter. Bowie was distraught in the wake of the breakup, which has been described as

DAVID BOWIE's career has been typified by innovation and experimentation. Constantly pushing the envelope, it brought him unparalleled critical and commercial acclaim from the 1960s onwards. He moved away from the astral hippie whimsy of his early albums and developed a rock-star persona and rock-band sound. His first chart entry was 1969's "Space Oddity," and only after his next hit (in 1972 as Ziggy Stardust with "Starman") was older material reissued. With the new sound emerged a new approach to lyric writing. Instead of straightforward description, he began to favor a more impressionistic, abstract style. He adopted a technique inspired by writer William Burroughs and also used by Bob Dylan, John Lennon, and others, which involved cutting words and phrases from newspapers and moving them around on his desk until they somehow fell into

place. So it was with "Life on Mars?," which first appeared on his 1971 LP, *Hunky Dory*. It performed better than its well-known follow-up, *The Rise and Fall of Ziggy Stardust and the Spiders from Mars*.

Bowie went on to have seven chart-topping albums over two decades, illustrating his longevity and ability to change and adapt. Musically, the contrast between "Life on Mars?" and "Let's Dance," a #1 single a decade later, shows his musical diversity and willingness to take risks.

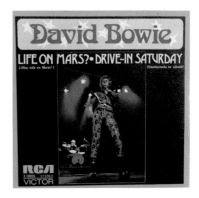

There was no sign of the William Burroughs technique of lyric writing in "Letter to Hermione," where Bowie sings that he tears his soul to cease the pain of missing her.

devastating by his many biographers. Bowie later wrote, "I was totally head-over-heels in love with her, and it really sort of demolished me.... It set me off on the 'Space Oddity' song." He documented his feelings overtly in "Letter to Hermione" and "An Occasional Dream," which appeared alongside "Space Oddity" on his album of the same name. They chart the end of any hope the young David Bowie might have retained of a reconciliation.

Hermione's last role was as Louise in *The Great Waltz*, a 1972 film biography of Johann Strauss the Younger; after that she disappeared from public view. Bowie claimed in later years, perhaps jokingly, that the girl with the mousy hair had married an anthropologist and gone to live in Irian Jawa, where she became a skilled cartographer, charting the rivers of New Guinea.

Life on Mars?

Lola
The Kinks

There are two different stories about the woman in the Kinks' sing-along hit "Lola," and neither of them is about the female of the species. The song is about a sexual encounter with a transvestite. So who was Lola? The more authentic but less glamorous answer is the one given in Jon Savage's official biography of the band. In it, Ray Davies recalls a late-night session while the Kinks were on tour. The band had made some new friends at a club earlier in the evening, and the party had moved from there back to the apartment of their manager, Robert Wace.

The night wore on and Wace spent much of it dancing with a black woman, muttering to Davies that "I'm really onto a thing here." Only at six the following morning, in the harsh light of dawn, did Davies comment on the shadow on the woman's chin. "Did you notice the stubble?" he asked his

Taking a walk on the wild side: Candy Darling has been the subject of many rock fantasies.

manager. "Yeah," replied Wace, rather the worse for wear—or, as Davies put it, "too pissed to care." "She" was a he.

Rolling Stone magazine claimed that its inspiration was the New York transvestite Candy Darling, whom Ray Davies had supposedly dated.

Candy, from Forest Hills, Queens, was born James Slattery in 1944. Darling became part of the colorful creative circle that revolved around Andy Warhol's Factory studio in New York City in the late 1960s. She appeared in two Warhol films, *Flesh* and *Women in Revolt* (originally simply called *Sex*). The Velvet Underground, who came to fame as the resident band at the Factory, wrote their song "Candy Says" about Ms. Darling's indecision over whether to have a sex change. And Velvet guitarist Lou Reed refers to her and several of the so-called Andy Warhol Superstars in his classic hymn to the times, "Walk on the Wild Side": "Candy came from out on the island / In the backroom she was everybody's darling."

Candy Darling is certainly a much more exotic source for the song, but the evidence for her involvement is slight. She conducted a lengthy interview with the singer in 1973 for Andy Warhol's *Interview* magazine. But the transcribed conversation is very superficially chatty and there is no mention of "Lola" or hint of any deeper intimacy.

Whatever the truth, "Lola" revitalized the Kinks' career. It updated their sound for a new decade and became a staple of their live sets from then on. Candy Darling died of leukemia in 1974. She left a note for Andy Warhol in which she declared, "Even with all my friends and my career on the upswing I felt too empty to go on in this unreal existence. I am just so bored by everything. You might say bored to death.... Did you know I couldn't last? I always knew it."

But she has been immortalized in song—by the Velvet Underground, Lou Reed, the Kinks, and, in 2004, by Morrissey on "You Know I Couldn't Last," a track from his album *You Are the Quarry*. A still of her from *Women in Revolt* is on the picture sleeve of the Smiths' 1987 single "Sheila Take a Bow," and a photograph by Peter Hujar of her on her deathbed graces the cover of the 2005 album "I Am a Bird Now" by Antony and the Johnsons.

THE KINKS were part of a wave of British music that "invaded" the U.S. in the 1960s. As a result they enjoyed more success in the U.S. than on home soil until they were banned from touring in the latter part of the 1960s. Led by brothers Ray and Dave Davies, the Kinks have been inducted into the Rock and Roll Hall of Fame. "Lola" was released in 1970 from the imaginatively titled album *Lola Versus Powerman and the Moneygoround, Part One*, which charted in the Top 40 in the U.S. but failed to chart in Britain.

Lovely Rita
The Beatles

Several years after "Lovely Rita" appeared on *Sergeant Pepper's Lonely Hearts Club Band*, traffic warden Meta Davies laid claim to immortality by nominating herself as the inspiration behind the song. In 1967, forty-six-year-old Meta's zone included the St. John's Wood area of London, where Abbey Road studios and Paul McCartney's flat are both situated. One day, early in the year, she booked a Beatle.

"His car was parked on a meter where the time had expired. I had to make out a ticket which, at the time, carried a 10 shilling fine. I'd just put it on the windscreen when Paul came along and took it off. He looked at it and read my signature which was in full, because there was another M Davies on the same unit. As he was walking away, he turned to me and said, 'Oh, is your name really Meta?' I told him that it was. We chatted

With the onset of Beatlemania, John, George, and Ringo moved out to leafy Surrey, while Paul bought a flat in St. John's Wood close to EMI's studio in Abbey Road—traffic warden Meta Davies' zone.

for a few minutes and he said, 'That would be a good name for a song. Would you mind if I use it?' And that was that. Off he went."

In keeping with the peace and love vibes of 1967, McCartney changed his original conception of "Lovely Rita": "I was thinking that it should be a hate song but then I thought that it would be better to love her." He subsequently explained further: "I'd been nicked a lot for parking, so the fun was to imagine one of them was an easy lay.... It somehow made them a figure of fun instead of a figure of terror and it was a way of getting me own back."

Traffic wardens had been around in England since 1960, but it was the terminology used in the United States that fascinated McCartney. "The phrase 'meter maid' was so American that it appealed, and to me a 'maid' was always a little sexy thing: 'Meter maid. Hey, come and check my meter, baby.' I saw a bit of that." He imagined a slightly kinky aspect to the character, that she might be "freaky too, like a military man, with a bag on her shoulders."

The song that emerged was a lighthearted lampoon, the story of a man trying to charm his way out of a parking fine.

McCartney clearly did not recall the incident to which Meta referred. "It wasn't based on a real person but, as often happened, it was claimed by a girl called Rita [sic] who was a traffic warden who apparently did give me a ticket, so that made the newspapers. I think it was more a question of coincidence: anyone called Rita who gave me a ticket would naturally think, 'It's me!' I didn't think, Wow, that woman gave me a ticket, I'll write a song about her—never happened like that."

Although Meta professed not to be a Beatles fan, someone close to her was. "My own daughter used to wait outside Abbey Road Studios to see them." She retired as a traffic warden in 1985, issuing her final ticket near to the famous recording complex.

THE BEATLES included "Lovely Rita" on *Sgt. Pepper's Lonely Hearts Club Band*, the most instantly recognizable of album titles. The album hit #1 in the U.S. in 1967, while also picking up four Grammys a year after it was released. Over time it was recognized as the greatest album of all time by *Rolling Stone* magazine and others. The song was never released as a single but, like many other tracks on the LP, became embedded in public consciousness anyway. *Sgt. Pepper* went eleven times platinum in the U.S., bettered only by later releases *The Beatles* and *Abbey Road*.

Lucy in the Sky with Diamonds
The Beatles

Lucy O'Donnell was just four years old when her nursery school classmate painted a picture of her, surrounded it with stars and shapes, and took it home to show his parents, John and Cynthia. "It's Lucy in the sky with diamonds," Julian Lennon told his father, providing the official inspiration for one of the Beatles' epic *Sgt. Pepper* songs.

Lucy and Julian were at Heath House nursery school in Weybridge, in Surrey's commuter belt. Lennon had moved out to exclusive St. George's Hill to get away from the screaming fans laying siege to the Beatles' London addresses. Even so, most of the children at nursery weren't dropped off in the morning in a chauffeur-driven psychedelic

John Lennon with son Julian Lennon, age four, at the time of his inspirational painting. The psychedelic Rolls was the most unusual of vehicles for the school drop-off.

Rolls Royce. "We were two very energetic school kids," Lucy said. "He would say 'Come on, Lucy', to get me to do things. He was the bravest boy in school whom I recall jumping into a freezing swimming pool."

John Lennon bought his son an unusual birthday present in 1967—his own gypsy caravan, complete with Sgt. Pepper *logo emblazoned on the back. It made a stir when it arrived in exclusive St. George's Hill.*

Given the spark of inspiration from Julian's painting, Lennon wove a psychedelic tale about the girl with kaleidoscope eyes under tangerine trees and marmalade skies. With controversy raging about the use of psychedelic drugs in the music business, the Beatles were keen to explain that the song was not about LSD, even though the lyrics had a hallucinatory quality all their own. And surely it was no surprise that Julian, the offspring of two art students, could come up with an artistic tour de force at the age of four.

In real life Lucy didn't much like the song that she allegedly inspired: "I don't feel I can relate to it. I just don't like it. I don't see a four-year-old kid running around with kaleidoscopic eyes. It doesn't make sense."

The tragedy was that the little girl in Julian Lennon's painting grew up with a love of children but couldn't have any of her own. She worked with special-needs children and ran a specialist nanny agency until she began to suffer from the autoimmune disease lupus in her thirties.

She married her childhood sweetheart, Ross Vodden, in 1996. Julian Lennon, whom she had seen only once since their nursery-school days while backstage after one of his solo concerts, sent his congratulations.

Julian, himself the subject of a Beatles song (Paul McCartney's "Hey Jude"), had his own happy nursery life disrupted soon after the release of *Sgt. Pepper.* John and Cynthia Lennon split up, and the painting that inspired his father has disappeared, although it was believed to be in Cynthia's possession at one time.

Lupus is a disease with symptoms that range from mild to severe. In 2009 the Voddens were on their first holiday in eight years when Lucy was taken ill with an infection—a serious incident for someone with no immune system. She was taken to hospital in Kings Lynn but died on September 29.

Maggie May
Rod Stewart

Rod Stewart borrowed the title of his breakthrough hit, "Maggie May," from a Liverpudlian sea shanty of the same name. The two songs share similar themes. The sailor's song concerns a prostitute who takes advantage of her client by stealing and selling his belongings while he sleeps. Stewart's hit is the tale of his regret at losing his virginity on a one-night stand with an unknown girl at the Beaulieu Jazz Festival in 1961. She stole his soul, and that was a pain he could do without.

It was in that same year of 1961 that Rod Stewart had his brief flirtation with professional soccer as an apprentice with Brentford FC. But he was young, his hormones were racing, and he resented the discipline required of an athlete. "A musician's life is a lot easier and I can also get drunk and make music, and I can't do that and play football." He quit the team, to the disgust of his father, a keen amateur soccer player (not a pool player, as the song suggests at one point). Later that year he took his first steps to enter the music business with an audition for the pioneering music producer Joe Meek, but for now he was content to be in the audience.

> Wake up Maggie
> I think I got something to say to you
> It's late September and I really should be back at school

Rod Stewart was 16 at the time, although the song itself wasn't written until 10 years later. In fact Rod had already left school the previous year. Furthermore the Beaulieu festival took place at the end of July, not in September. It was a groundbreaking event, which set the template for pop festivals to the present day—carnival atmosphere, fairground rides, camping, alternative lifestyle, amplification, crash tents. Headliners in 1961 were Chris Barber, Kenny Ball, and the late Johnny Dankworth, between them representing the ancient and modern in the jazz scene. It was a bold program—the previous year there had been a full-blown riot at the festival between modernist Johnny Dankworth's fans and those of traditional jazz musician Acker Bilk, who were known as ravers. Perhaps the potential for

Stewart's breakthrough third solo album, **Every Picture Tells a Story,** *spawned the singles "Maggie May," "Reason to Believe," and "I'm Losing You."*

such anarchy was part of the attraction for some of the audience in 1961.

A Movietone newsreel reported on the festival that year by declaring that "fans forget the conventional life ... and act like crazy!" Clearly Rod Stewart was swept up in the mood of the event. "It was a jazz festival. I was a virgin, and this girl got a hold of me—I think she was in her thirties—and, like nowadays, everyone was in tents.... She took me to hers and had her way with me!" he recalled in a television interview in 2009.

In reality, Maggie (assuredly not her real name) seems to have given Rod a taste for such pleasures. There was a strong link at the time between jazz fans and the Campaign for Nuclear Disarmament; according to biographers Rod took part in the annual Aldermaston, England, antinuclear marches from 1961 to 1963. He was arrested three times at sit-ins, but his commitment to protest may not have been entirely political; by all accounts, he found that being part of the CND movement was an excellent way to meet girls.

ROD STEWART made his name with the Jeff Beck Group and then the Faces, before embarking on a solo career that would make him a global success. "Maggie May" was his breakthrough single, charting at #1 in the U.S. and the U.K. It was included on his first #1 album, *Every Picture Tells a Story.* He used this early success as the springboard to launch his career in the U.S.; further releases like "Tonight's the Night (Gonna Be Alright)," "Do Ya Think I'm Sexy?" and "Have I Told You Lately" would top the charts in the U.S. while a string of platinum-selling albums at the turn of the millennium saw him tackling numbers from the Great American Songbook. Now in his fifth decade as a performer and musician, Stewart has cemented his reputation as one of Britain's best: his twenty-fifth studio album, *Stardust,* reached the Top 10 in the U.K. and America in 2004.

Maybe I'm Amazed
Paul McCartney

The daughter of a wealthy New York lawyer, Linda Eastman was in London in May 1967 to take photographs of rock musicians for publisher Bantam Books. She accompanied members of the Animals to the Bag O'Nails nightclub to see Georgie Fame perform. She was accustomed to being around famous musicians, so meeting Paul McCartney was unlikely to faze her.

Linda recalled that "we flirted a bit" before Paul asked her to go to another club with him and his friends. They met again a few days later at the launch party for the album *Sgt. Pepper's Lonely Hearts Club Band*, which was at Beatles' manager Brian Epstein's Belgravia residence. Shortly afterward, Linda flew home to New York. At the time, Paul was still involved with actress Jane Asher, but the relationship was faltering, as Jane was unwilling to give up her career for him.

The chemistry between Paul and Linda was evident at the launch party for **Sgt. Pepper.**

When McCartney visited New York in April 1968 with John Lennon to launch the Beatles' Apple Corps organization, he renewed his acquaintance with Linda. With Asher finally out of the picture, he invited Linda to stay with him in London in September. She immediately jumped on a transatlantic flight, arriving at his St. John's Wood residence. Linda found herself alone as Paul was in Abbey Road studios for a late-night recording session with the Beatles. Linda recalled being "in someone else's house, somebody I didn't even know that well. This was, like, a freaky experience but I took it in my stride because I did a lot of things like that during this period."

The following March, they were married when Linda was four months pregnant with their first child, Mary. It was the second time around for Linda, who already had a seven-year-old daughter, Heather. "I wasn't looking for another marriage," she said. "I had been married before.... But Paul and I married because of convention."

The simple, heartfelt lyric of "Maybe I'm Amazed" relates how Linda helped him through the protracted and messy process of the Beatles' breakup, with all its personal and financial complications.

> Baby I'm a man and maybe I'm a lonely man
> Who's in the middle of something
> That he doesn't really understand

He later recalled that the song was written for "me and Linda, with the Beatles breaking up that was my feeling. Maybe I'm amazed at what's going on, maybe I'm not but maybe I am. 'Maybe I'm amazed at the way you pulled me out of time, hung me on the line.' There were things happening at the time and these phrases were my symbols for them." Paul later added that "every love song I write is for Linda."

The McCartneys were constant companions for the next 29 years. At Paul's insistence, the self-professed nonmusician Linda joined his band, Wings. According to Linda, "We spend so much time together because that's how we like it. I never used to go on girls' nights out, even at school. And Paul has never liked going out for a night with the boys."

Linda McCartney died of breast cancer in April 1998 at age 56. She was as famous for her antivivisection views and vegetarian lifestyle as for marrying a Beatle.

PAUL McCARTNEY has to be considered one of the most influential British musicians of all time, both as a solo act and a member of the Beatles. His success has been unparalleled, and *The Guinness Book of Records* lists him as the most successful musician and composer in popular music history. "Maybe I'm Amazed" appeared on McCartney's eponymous debut LP in 1970, but was not released as a single. A live version of the track was released seven years later by his band Wings; it reached the U.S. Top 10, proving the song's enduring popularity.

Miss Amanda Jones
The Rolling Stones

Mystery surrounds the early life of Amanda Lear. She was born between 1939 and 1946, most likely in Hong Kong, though Provence and Saigon are also possible. But the most enduring enigma is whether Amanda entered the world as a male, a subject into which she has consistently refused to be drawn. When asked during a television interview, "Were you born a man?" she replied, "No, I was born a baby."

The longtime muse of Salvador Dalí (right), Amanda Lear dines in Paris in the 1960s with the Spanish surrealist painter and actor Yul Brynner (left).

The story goes that her original name was Alain Tapp; she appeared in cabaret in Paris between 1958 and 1959, as a showgirl called Peki d'Oslo in a transvestite revue. Around this time, she began taking hormones in preparation for a sex-change operation, which took place in Casablanca, Morocco, in 1963. This may or may not have been paid for by Spanish surrealist painter Salvador Dalí.

In 1964, she was in London studying art at St. Martin's College. She is said to have paid a fellow student named Lear £50 to marry her so she could obtain British citizenship. Back in Paris the following year, Amanda renewed her acquaintance with Dalí, becoming a constant companion of the painter and his wife, Gala, for the next two decades. After being "discovered" on the streets of Paris in 1965, she launched a ten-year career in fashion modeling.

In London, Lear dated Guinness heir and friend of the stars Tara Browne, the inspiration for the Beatles' "A Day in the Life." She was frequently seen enjoying the high life with Rolling Stone Brian Jones, whom she met through Mick Jagger's girlfriend Marianne Faithfull. Lear was one of many women romantically linked with Jones, although he was in a tempestuous relationship with Anita Pallenberg at the time.

By the time "Miss Amanda Jones," written by Mick Jagger and Keith Richards, was recorded in August 1966, Brian Jones was becoming a peripheral figure in the band he had formed. He finally left the Stones in 1969, drowning in the swimming pool at his home shortly afterwards. Jagger's sarcastic lyric is ambiguous; its references to "family," "nobility," and "of her lineage she's rightfully proud," could equally apply to a debutante as to Amanda Lear and her murky past. Combing Jones's and Lear's names, the song plays not only on rumors of her transsexuality but also on Brian's androgynous looks. There are further ambivalent lines:

> Hey girl your suspender shows
> And the girl behind you looks a bit unsure
> She looks quite delightfully stoned
> She's the darling of the discotheque crowd

Lear insists that it was she and Salvador Dalí who concocted the rumors of her transsexual status to launch her musical career in the 1970s. "Everything Dalí said, I just listened to. He was the genius, who was I? When it came to launching my career, he told me I was a lousy singer and if I wanted to sell records, I'd have to find something other than the music to attract people to buy them. So we built the Amanda

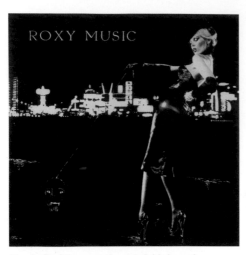

One half of the evocative gatefold sleeve for Roxy Music's **For Your Pleasure** *album.*

Lear persona into something very intriguing and very ambiguous and it worked."

In 1973 Lear was briefly engaged to Bryan Ferry of Roxy Music and, that same year, appeared on the cover of the band's second album, *For Your Pleasure*. The image she portrayed, leading a black panther on a leash while posing in a skin-tight leather dress, brought Lear plenty of exposure. She quickly capitalized on this by appearing in the live performance of David Bowie's 1973 hit song "Sorrow" in his *1980 Floor Show* stage production. This was televised in the United States by NBC for the TV series *Midnight Special* in November 1973, and her appearance is often referred to as the official launch of Lear's career in music. (She is also said to have had an affair with Bowie.)

Lear would become the darling of the discotheque crowd when she embarked on her own recording career in 1975. She achieved huge popularity in Europe as a singer, becoming a gay disco icon before briefly leaving music behind and becoming a household name in Italy as a television host. She worked for four years as a TV entertainer for the Italian Canale 5 and French La Cinq channels, but also continued to pursue her self-confessed greatest passion, art. From the mid-1980s she exhibited her work in major galleries all over the world.

Lear joined the French aristocracy in 1979 by marrying Alain-Philippe Malagnac d'Argens de Villèle. The ceremony took place in Las Vegas just three weeks after the couple first met at fashionable discothèque Le Palace, the Paris equivalent of Studio 54.

A musical comeback in 1987 was cut short when Lear was seriously injured in a car accident and had to spend months convalescing. While in hospital she began work on a novel, *L'Immortelle*. In 2000 Lear's husband died in a house fire; after mourning him, she returned to work with a vengeance.

In July 2006, Lear was awarded the title of Chevalier dans l'Ordre

Amanda Lear with Princess Stephanie and Prince Albert of Monaco, attending the thirty-first International Circus Festival held in Monaco in 2006.

National des Arts et des Lettres by the French Ministry of Culture in recognition of having "significantly contributed to the enrichment of the French cultural inheritance." Controversially, the name appearing on the honors list was "Mme Amanda Tapp dite Amanda Lear"—the first time the French authorities had publicly confirmed Lear's birth name, something she herself had, until then, denied.

THE ROLLING STONES included "Miss Amanda Jones" on the album *Between the Buttons*, which, released in 1967, reached the Top 3 in both the U.K. and the U.S. "Let's Spend the Night Together" was the LP's most successful single in the U.K., reaching #3, but "Ruby Tuesday" was included in the U.S. version of the album and topped the charts there when released on 45.

Their Satanic Majesties Request was released at the end of the year and performed similarly, charting at #3 in the U.K. and #2 in the States, though it was considered a poor relation of the Beatles' *Sgt. Pepper*. Two years later the Stones would step it up a notch with their 1969 effort *Let It Bleed*. It would begin a string of chart-topping LPs on both sides of the Atlantic.

Moses
Coldplay

cademy Award–winner Gwyneth Paltrow became one of the most recognizable names in Hollywood after starring in Oscar-winning films such as *Seven* and *Shakespeare in Love*. It had been her role with Brad Pitt in 1995's *Seven* that set tongues wagging. They soon became showbiz's number-one couple. They split in 1997.

Paltrow met British musician Chris Martin, lead singer of Coldplay, backstage at a concert in London in October 2002. Rumor has it that Paltrow was impressed by the show but even more impressed with the band's frontman. His vegetarianism and championing of political causes such as fair trade clearly appealed to the actress.

Days later, British tabloid newspaper the *Sun* carried confirmation of an embryonic relationship. "I'm proud to be with someone who's very nice and very beautiful but she's not my girlfriend at the moment," Martin revealed. "I feel out of my depth with all this. I met her for the first time at our gig at Wembley two weeks ago. It's early days. I got her number, rang her and asked if she wanted to meet. We went out at the weekend and we seem to get on. We met up as friends and nothing has happened. We had a good time, though. I don't know when we're going out again."

The following month, *The Sun* reported Paltrow was telling friends that Martin was the love of her life.

By April 2003 Paltrow was following his band around the world as unobtrusively as possible, though she was also shooting a new movie, *The World of Tomorrow*, in London. "Gwyneth is always running around after him," a source told *Us Weekly*. "She tries to keep out of the limelight, but she's always in the wings waiting."

British producer Alison Owen, a close friend of Paltrow's since 1995's *Moonlight and Valentino*, confirmed that "she's very happy in her personal life…. Gwyneth makes judgments about someone very quickly, very instinctively and decides whether she likes or dislikes them. She's very instinctive about who she places her trust in, and once she makes up her mind it's difficult for her to change it."

The pair were highly secretive, not allowing any media intrusion to

Moses was Gwyneth Paltrow's second child with Coldplay singer Chris Martin.

trickle into their private life, and they wed in an unpublicized ceremony in California in December 2003. Although they married in the U.S., the couple would make London their home.

Their first child, daughter Apple, was born in 2004, finally creating a family for Paltrow after false starts with Pitt and with fellow actor Ben Affleck.

In 2006, Paltrow and Martin welcomed their second child, Moses, naming him after the song Martin had written for his future wife shortly before their wedding. Before playing it at a gig in Sydney he announced, "This is a song about falling in love with the most beautiful woman in the world."

Paltrow scaled down her work schedule after Moses's birth, claiming it was her own decision; her biggest role since becoming a mother of two would come in 2008's *Marvel* comic remake of *Iron Man*.

It appeared the arrival of their new baby had caused the couple to temporarily let down their walls and give the public a brief glance into their lives—for the length of one song at least.

COLDPLAY has become arguably the most popular British rock band of a generation. Perhaps significantly, the track "Moses" was not released on a regular studio album and could only be obtained as an exclusive track on their *Live 2003* CD, recorded during an Australian concert. They went on to score transatlantic #1s with *X&Y* and *Viva La Vida or Death and All His Friends*, the latter winning them three Grammys.

Mrs. Potter's Lullaby
Counting Crows

Despite starring in films like *Con Air* and *Along Came a Spider*, Cleveland-born actress Monica Potter has been considered by some critics as a poor man's Julia Roberts. She admitted, "I usually get the scripts that have Cameron Diaz, Jennifer Aniston, Drew Barrymore or Julia Roberts' fingerprints on them."

But when Counting Crows' dreadlocked frontman and songwriter Adam Duritz watched her in 1998's poorly received comedy-drama *Patch Adams*, he was so infatuated he went on to write a song about being romantically involved with her—and life soon imitated art.

The rocker from Baltimore, Maryland, already had a reputation for snaring the A-list ladies, having already reportedly dated *Friends* stars Courteney Cox and Jennifer Aniston.

Their brief romance began as a blind date, after Duritz mentioned the song he had penned. Potter remembers: "He wrote this song about me and told someone about it and I was so flattered because I had just gotten divorced and it was a very bad time. It was about him seeing a girl on the screen, it's more about him. Potter is my married name. I didn't change it because it's my kids' name, plus it flows." (Her maiden name was Brokaw.)

She was seemingly unimpressed and questioned the real meaning of the song; thus it was unsurprising the relationship was not long-term. "We dated for three or four months, then I moved my kids back to Cleveland. We were better friends."

There are parts of the track that unmistakably depict obsession with an actress on the silver screen, be it Potter or otherwise.

> Well I know I don't know you
> And you're probably not what you seem
> Oh but I'd sure like to find out
> So why don't you climb down off that movie screen?

The attraction for Duritz, who suffers from depression, could have been falling for a complex character that meets a tragic end, such as

Monica Potter was curious and "flattered" when she heard the song written for her.

Potter's character, Carin, in *Patch Adams*. If only gaining the affections of your favorite movie star was as easy as writing a song, then men across the country would surely be picking up their pens en masse.

As for Monica Potter, she married orthopedic surgeon Daniel Christopher Allison in June 2005. Potter and Allison had a daughter in August 2005; since then, she has returned to television and movie acting. In 2009, Potter became a cast member of a new TV series called *Trust Me*, a modern-day equivalent of the AMC hit *Mad Men*. *Trust Me* revolved around a fictional advertising agency and Potter's character, Sarah Krajicek-Hunter. The show was canceled after the first season due to poor ratings.

COUNTING CROWS formed in California in 1991, clearly influenced by rock groups REM and Nirvana. But they went on to make their own name, selling more than twenty million records. "Mrs. Potter's Lullaby" failed to make the charts when it was released in 1999. However, it was featured on their third studio album, *This Desert Life*, which made #8 in the U.S., and the Top 20 in the U.K. The track came immediately after the band's highest-charting U.S. single, "Hanginaround."

Counting Crows went on to gain further exposure and an Oscar nomination for "Accidentally in Love," which featured in the Disney film *Shrek 2* in 2004. *Saturday Nights & Sunday Mornings*, their fifth LP, reached #3 in the U.S. album charts in 2008.

My Sharona
The Knack

The irresistible rhythm and energetic vocals of the Knack's debut single, "My Sharona," have guaranteed it a permanent place in rock's history. It even made it onto George W. Bush's iPod. It's a favorite of aspiring bass players everywhere and an easy framework for a seemingly endless list of clever lyrical parodies by satirists and advertisers: "My Toyota," "My Corona," "My Bologna," "My Payola," "Ay-atollah"—they've all been done and more. But beneath the bright, uptempo beat, the lyrics reveal a tale of lust and longing: "Never gonna stop, give it up / Such a dirty mind / Always get it up for the touch of the younger kind."

The words document the lustful obsession of twenty-seven-year-old lead singer Doug Fieger with a sixteen-year-old Los Angeles schoolgirl, Sharona Alperin. She worked part-time in a clothing store, where Fieger was introduced to her by his girlfriend of the time. As he reminisced in later years, "She had an overpowering scent, and it drove me crazy."

He was persistent in his pursuit of her. When legendary producer Mike Chapman was recording the song for the band's first album, Fieger brought Sharona into the studio on backing vocals (reportedly joining with others on a background chant of "F***-a-me," placed very low in the final mix). He put her on the cover of the single. He encouraged her to leave her then boyfriend. And in the wake of the song's top-of-the-chart success, he sent seventeen-year-old Sharona a ticket to join the band on tour in Hawaii.

There, finally, they became romantically involved. And despite the age difference, the relationship seems to have been successful. They stayed together for four years, during which she inspired many of Fieger's compositions. They were for a while engaged, and even after they separated she remained his friend and muse. In 2009 Doug revealed that the song "You Gotta Be There" from the Knack's 1999 album *Zoom* was about Sharona.

Alperin's subsequent professional career has built on her time with Fieger. "When Doug was looking for houses, he was always on tour, so ... I'd choose five houses and then show him. One of the agents said to me, I've never seen anyone show houses like you: you should be an agent." After they split, she earned her real-estate license. She now works for Sotheby's and specializes in finding homes for celebrity clients from the entertainment industry. Her list is confidential but is known to include Leonardo di Caprio. "My Sharona" plays on the homepage of her Web site.

Sharona Alperin not only inspired the single, she featured on the single sleeve, too.

Both Sharona and Doug subsequently got married, although Doug's marriage ended in divorce after ten years. In 2006 he developed a brain tumor, and in 2007 was diagnosed with lung cancer. Both his ex-wife and Sharona tended to his care during his long battle with the illness, a remarkable sign of the lasting affection he inspired.

In the end, he lost the battle on February 14, 2010. Sharona was at his deathbed. His passing sparked renewed interest in both the woman and the song more than thirty years after Fieger first declared his love for her in the most public of ways. "Doug changed my life forever," says Sharona. "It was incredibly, incredibly exciting—a very special experience. You could not escape putting on the radio and hearing 'My Sharona' ... But I was never, never sick of the song."

THE KNACK rose to prominence in the late 1970s amid a music scene saturated with disco. "My Sharona" was their debut offering, and, riding the briefly popular power-pop wave, it soared to #1 on the Billboard Hot 100. Unfortunately for the band they would struggle to ever match the success of their phenomenal first single. Though their second release, "Good Girls Don't,"

reached #9, none of their next singles managed to break into the Top 20. They disbanded in 1982 but reunited in 1997 after a series of failed attempts; the only absent member was drummer Bruce Gary, who died in 2006.

The band played on, but even before Doug Fieger's death in 2010, the heady days of a #1 hit single seemed even further than three decades away.

Our House
Crosby, Stills, Nash & Young

In the summer of 1968 everybody who was anybody in the West Coast music scene lived in Laurel Canyon. The Canyon was a Los Angeles neighborhood that had always been home to artists of one sort or another: Harry Houdini and Clara Bow in the 1920s, Mary Astor and Boris Karloff in the 1930s, Leslie Caron and Errol Flynn in the 1950s.

In the late 1960s it was colonized by the rising stars of hippie counterculture. Frank Zappa, (Mama) Cass Elliot, Jimi Hendrix, Carole King, members of Canned Heat, the Doors, the Byrds, the Monkees, and Buffalo Springfield—they all lived there. So too did the emerging voice of her generation, Joni Mitchell.

Joni Mitchell's house on Lookout Mountain Road was the hub for a close-knit circle of folk-rock musicians who would gather around the brick fireplace in her living room, squatting on cushions on the warm wooden floor, exchanging ideas and songs long into the night.

> Staring at the fire
> For hours and hours
> While I listen to you
> Play your love songs
> All night long for me
> Only for me

At one such party Stephen Stills (an ex–Buffalo Springfield member) and David Crosby (an ex-Byrds member, producer, and ex-lover of Joni Mitchell) were playing a song they had been working on, "You Don't Have to Cry," for the assembled guests. Among those present was Graham Nash, on vacation from Britain where he was the lead singer with the Hollies, and he was in the process of falling in love with Joni Mitchell. He was entranced by the music and by their harmonies; he asked them to sing it again several times before suddenly joining in with an immaculate third harmony in his distinctive high tenor.

It was a thunderbolt moment. The rest of Joni's guests that night fell into a stunned silence. Stills and Crosby had been searching for a third

Lovers Graham Nash and Joni Mitchell share some quality time in the back of a limo on the way to Big Bear Lake, 1969.

person to join their new project; in that moment they became Crosby, Stills & Nash, the pinnacle of the 1960s folk-country-rock movement. With the addition the following year of fellow ex-Buffalo Neil Young, they would come to define the genre.

Graham Nash quit the Hollies, joined Crosby and Stills, and moved in with Joni Mitchell. It was a heady time. Mitchell was working on her next album, *Clouds*, and Nash was writing songs for what would be the classic folk-rock album *Déjà Vu*. Nash said that, in the Nash-Mitchell household, they competed to "[get] to the piano first." They were considered a golden couple among their peers; it was said that the room lit up when they walked in.

They were in the habit of going to breakfast at a deli on Ventura Boulevard, and after one such occasion, returning to the car, they passed a little antique store. Graham described what happened: "There was this beautiful vase, and Joni loved it … so she bought the vase and we took it back…. It was one of those L.A. mornings that are grey and not quite rainy…and I said to her, Why don't you put some flowers in the vase and I'll light a fire? … and I started to think, God, that's an incredibly domestic scene…. I love this woman, and this moment is a very grounded moment in our relationship. I sat down at the piano, and an hour later 'Our House' was done."

> I'll light the fire
> And you place the flowers in the jar
> That you bought today

What's particularly interesting about the song "Our House" is that it shows his longing for a very old-fashioned kind of domestic bliss. The free love of his new hippie world, celebrated all around him in life and song, even in other tracks on *Déjà Vu*, was not for him.

A photograph of Joni Mitchell from 1971, taken near her Laurel Canyon home.

This was not Joni's vision of happiness. For her, domesticity (particularly for a woman) meant the abandonment of dreams in favor of drudgery and subservience. Mitchell had grown up watching her grandmother suppress her own creative urges in order to be a wife and mother, and she had no intention of going down that road.

Despite their obvious love for each other, Graham wanted too conventional a relationship, and Joni was too afraid of having to suppress her muse for it to work out. She was in love with Graham but couldn't make it work on his terms, nor could he on hers. By the end of 1969 it was over.

Both performers have continued to record and release albums into the twenty-first century. Both have also pursued parallel careers in the visual arts. Nash has had a lifelong interest in photography. Mitchell is a fine painter, whose works have graced her own and other artist's album covers since the 1960s.

Graham Nash married actress Susan Sennett in 1977. They are still married. Joni Mitchell has been romantically linked to many musicians, and eventually married her producer and bass player, Larry Klein, in 1982. Although the marriage was dissolved in 1994, they remain on good terms and continue to work together professionally.

Mitchell wrote her own view of her relationship with Nash in the song "Willy" on her first gold album, 1970's *Ladies of the Canyon*. Willy was Graham's nickname.

Her career was indeed just taking off, and she was in no mood to be smothered or hidden. Looking back, Nash likened the house they shared to the 1945 British romantic film *Enchanted Cottage*, in which two damaged people, hiding from the world, fall in love and find that all their scars become invisible, at least to each other. "The house reminded me of that house [the enchanted cottage]; once you walked in through that front door, everything disappeared."

CROSBY, STILLS, NASH & YOUNG made a good thing even better when they followed up CS&N's eponymous #6 1969 debut album. Recruiting Neil Young just in time for Woodstock, they released *Déjà Vu* in the spring of 1970 and saw it top the U.S. chart—as did its live follow-up, *Four Way Street* (1971). On the latter, the pressure to include solo and group material was so great that "Our House" had to be left off. The song enjoyed unexpected additional exposure in the first decade of the twenty-first century when a U.K. bank used it as the theme for a commercial to sell mortgages—not, perhaps, what Graham Nash had in mind when he first penned it.

Peggy Sue
Buddy Holly

Peggy Sue Gerron was the girlfriend of Buddy Holly's drummer and best friend, Jerry Allison. She became the inspiration for the singer's classic song, which was the follow-up to his 1957 single "That'll Be the Day."

As Ms. Gerron recalls, inspiration struck the bespectacled pop bard "sometime during the middle of the night. He got Norman Petty, the producer, [on the phone] and he told him, 'I've written this song and I've named it after Jerry's girlfriend.'" Holly and Petty share the songwriting credits, though how much each one contributed is uncertain.

Peggy Sue (front) with Richie Valens' "Donna" in 1994.

Holly had already met Peggy Sue at a high-school gig he performed in Sacramento, California, when, late for the show, he sent her flying. "He ran over to me, guitar in one hand, amp in the other, and said, 'I don't have time to pick you up, but you sure are pretty," before he ran off. Three weeks later, she was on a date with future husband Jerry Allison when he introduced her to his friend. "[Buddy] started laughing, Jerry asked him what was so funny, and he said 'I've already overwhelmed your Peggy Sue.'"

Holly's death in a plane crash while on tour made him one of rock music's first immortals. Jerry Allison had quit the band before that last tour, and the couple was staying with Holly's parents. As Peggy Sue recalls, "Somebody called the house and told us the Crickets were dead, so Jerry made some calls," remembers Ms. Gerron. "It turned out Mr. and Mrs. Holley didn't know, they actually heard about it on the radio."

Yet "American Pie" songsmith Don McLean's pronouncement that February 3, 1959, was "the day the music died" turned out to be wrong; Buddy's total of posthumous U.K. hits exceed his score when alive by a factor of more than three to one. Ms. Gerron's name appears in not one but two song titles, the other being "Peggy Sue Got Married." Striking a more melancholy note than its predecessor, it was recorded by Holly on a home tape recorder in 1958 and only heard after his death.

Following her split from Jerry Allison in the mid-1960s, Peggy Sue went to college in California and became a dental assistant. She married again, had two children, and helped her husband establish a plumbing business, becoming the first licensed woman plumber in California.

She published an autobiography, *Whatever Happened to Peggy Sue?* in 2008 to celebrate the fiftieth anniversary of "Peggy Sue" reaching the charts. Gerron said material for the book came from about 150 diary entries she made during the time she knew Buddy Holly. "I wanted to give him his voice," she said. "It's my book, my memoirs. We were very, very good friends. He was probably one of the best friends I ever had."

However, Buddy Holly's widow was unhappy: "It's very interesting that this woman makes up all these stories," Maria Elena Holly said from her home in Dallas. "He never, never considered Peggy Sue a friend." She said her husband changed the name to Peggy Sue after Jerry Allison asked him to. Buddy's brother, Larry, maintains the name Holly originally intended to use was that of his niece, Cindy Lou.

BUDDY HOLLY's career at the top only lasted 18 months; yet he managed to influence a generation of rock 'n' roll performers well after his life was tragically cut short. Paul McCartney once said, "If it wasn't for the Crickets, there wouldn't be any Beatles." They were the first self-contained rock 'n' roll band that wrote and played their own songs. More than that, they pioneered overdubbing and multi-track recording years before it became standard practice. "Peggy Sue" was released in late 1957; Holly's popularity was already at fever pitch, as he had found success with "That'll Be the Day." The newer song was credited to him alone rather than the Crickets due to two parallel record deals with Brunswick and Coral.

Philadelphia Freedom
Elton John

If you went out and bought a copy of Elton John's latest single, "Philadelphia Freedom," in March 1975, you were no doubt delighted with Elton's first venture into dance music. You were probably pretty pleased with the B-side too, a live duet with John Lennon of the Beatles' classic "I Saw Her Standing There." You might also have been intrigued to read on the A-side label the dedication "to B.J.K."

At the start of 1975 Elton John was firing on all cylinders. In the previous two years, four successive albums had reached #1 in the British, U.S., Canadian, and Australian charts. His talent and high earnings allowed him to join the ranks of pop royalty, and he was mixing in circles of the rich, privileged, and famous. Elton is a star who understands the power of success, not only to open doors but also to do good in the world. His friendship with tennis star Billie Jean King is a case in point.

Elton had met Ms. King at a celebrity party in 1973, a couple of weeks before the celebrated Battle of the Sexes tennis match challenge in which she defeated Bobby Riggs. Riggs was a former world tennis number one and Wimbledon champion, who had taken it on himself to spout the chauvinist line that women's tennis was so inferior to men's that even he, a fifty-five-year-old has-been, could beat the best of the current female players. King, a vocal advocate of equal prize money for women in the major tournaments, won the match in straight sets.

At the party, each was too starstruck by the other to dare strike up a conversation. "Elton's a favorite," Billie Jean recalled later, "but we were both too shy to say hello." After an approach by one of Elton's "people" however, the two immediately hit it off and agreed to meet again at Wimbledon the following year.

Elton no doubt admired Billie Jean's campaigning spirit, of which he himself possessed plenty. He was in any case a great sports fan who would, a few years later, buy his own beloved Watford Football Club. During the year that followed that first meeting, he was particularly thrilled to play against Ms. King for a few minutes at a charity tennis event. By the time they met again in 1974, he was an avid follower of

Portrait of Billie Jean taken during the Virginia Slims of Denver tournament in Colorado, August 1973. She won her fifth Wimbledon title that year, defeating Chris Evert.

Billie Jean King's team in the World Tennis League. The team was called the Philadelphia Freedoms. During Wimbledon 1974, Elton John called on Billie Jean King as arranged. "He came over in the Rolls," she says, "and we talked and talked, and listened to music. He finally said, I'd like to write you a song." Billie Jean was incredulous, but Elton insisted that he owed it to her for the privilege of having played tennis against her.

She assumed that it was a friendly but casual remark that would come to nothing, but Elton had got hold of the idea and took it to his lyricist, Bernie Taupin. Taupin is reported to have protested that he couldn't write a song about tennis or, for that matter, one with such an awkward title as "Philadelphia Freedom." But he set to work. What emerged was not a sporting anthem but a celebration of perseverance and teamwork.

As Taupin says of "Philadelphia Freedom," "fifty per cent of the people who liked it never even listened to the words." People buy dance records, he believes, because "it's got a good beat man, yeah—I can dance to that. The words, at least in the beginning, are secondary."

On the musical side, Elton picked up on a happy coincidence—the popularity at the time of the Philadelphia sound in soul music, pioneered by the hit-writing team of Gamble and Huff and their record label, Philadelphia International.

A few weeks later he made his way sheepishly to Ms. King's locker room at the tournament in which she was playing, carrying a tape recorder. Nervously he pressed play and waited for her reaction. She loved it. The record was released in March 1975 and went to #1 in the U.S. and Canada. Its relatively poor showing in Britain (#12) may be because, under Musicians' Union rules at the time, string sections had to be re-recorded by British musicians. Elton refused to allow this, claiming that British players could not do justice to Gene Page's Philly sound.

Over the years, the song has inevitably become an unofficial anthem for the city of Philadelphia. The friendship between King and John that

ELTON JOHN, one of the most successful singer-songwriters of all time, was already immensely popular when he released "Philadelphia Freedom" in 1975. It was later included as a bonus track on his ninth studio album, *Captain Fantastic and the Brown Dirt Cowboy*, which debuted at #1 on the *Billboard* pop chart the same year. His piano-based rock 'n' roll had catapulted him to iconic status in both the U.K. and America, but after 1975 he dispensed with the services of original band members Dee Murray and Nigel Olsson, and the hits declined. He went on to have the biggest selling single of all time when he re-recorded "Candle in the Wind" in memory of Princess Diana in 1997—the song sold more than thirty-five million copies worldwide. As well as lending his hand to musical soundtracks, including Disney's *The Lion King*, Sir Elton spent the late 1990s and 2000s performing duets with contemporary artists such as 2Pac and the Killers.

led to its original composition has gone from strength to strength. Every year they cohost an annual pro-am tennis event, WTT Smash Hits, to raise money for AIDS charities, including John's own Elton John AIDS Foundation, of which King is a chairperson.

Billie Jean King is considered one of the greatest tennis players of all time, man or woman. She eventually retired from competitive tennis in 1990, only to turn to coaching U.S. national teams to victory instead. She is the founder of the Women's Sports Foundation and the Women's Tennis Association, and continues to campaign actively against sexism wherever it occurs in sport and in society at large.

Elton's love for tennis—and Billie Jean King—is second only to his love of soccer. Elton has long been associated with Watford Football Club near his home town of Pinner.

The Prettiest Star
David Bowie

Nineteen-year-old Mary Angela Barnett met David Bowie in 1969 through Calvin Mark Lee. Lee worked for the British arm of Mercury Records, with whom Bowie was trying to secure a new recording contract.

Angela was born in Cyprus; her father was a former U.S. Army colonel of British descent, while her mother was Polish. She had attended an exclusive Swiss boarding school before being sent to Connecticut College for Women at sixteen; she later got expelled for having a very public affair with a fellow female student. Escorted to London by her mother, she enrolled first at a secretarial college, then at Kingston Polytechnic, but she quickly abandoned the student lifestyle in favor of something more exciting.

Calvin took Angela to see Bowie perform at the Roundhouse in January 1969. She recalled being entranced by his stage presence and "a voice so compelling that no one could turn a head. David captivated every single member of the audience." They were briefly introduced backstage, although it was not until April that

Angie Bowie sees husband David off at Victoria Station, London, July 1973.

their relationship began in earnest. After dinner, the three attended the debut of progressive-rock pioneers King Crimson at London's Speakeasy Club. The very next day, she and David became lovers; according to Angela, "It seemed predestined."

Over the coming months, Angela became an increasingly crucial figure in David's life, providing behind-the-scenes promotion for his career, as well as moral support. She was openly bisexual and encouraged him to follow her lead by becoming weirder and more outrageous. Theirs was an open relationship, each acknowledging the other's freedom to sleep with different partners.

By Christmas, the couple was living together in Haddon Hall, a large Victorian house in Beckenham, Kent. David's mother made her disapproval clear in no uncertain terms to Angela: "She didn't like her son living in sin—it wasn't respectable." To escape the situation, Angela flew to Cyprus to visit her parents during the festive period. David sent a card containing a scribbled note: "Please come back. We will marry, I promise, later this year." The card was delayed by a postal strike and, anxious at having received no response, he called her and, "into the telephone, he played the acetate of a new song he had composed for me. It was called 'The Prettiest Star.'"

Their wedding took place at Beckenham Registry Office in March 1970. David and Angela exchanged Peruvian bangles in place of the traditional rings. By then "The Prettiest Star" had been recorded and released. It featured David's old friend and glam rival Marc Bolan on lead guitar, but the session had ended on a sour note, with Marc's wife, June, stating that her husband was "too good" for Bowie. Angela consoled David and assured him that one day he would have a guitarist of his own.

She was right; Bowie soon began working with Mick Ronson, a talented player and arranger who would be his musical right-hand man for the next few years. David's 1973 album, *Aladdin Sane*, featured a re-recorded version of "The Prettiest Star" with Ronson playing lead guitar. This version is better known than the original single, which reputedly sold fewer than a thousand copies. David had insisted on releasing "The Prettiest Star" as the follow-up to his first hit, "Space Oddity," overriding his manager's objection that it was not sufficiently commercial.

As Bowie achieved the kind of success and acclaim that he, and Angela, had always craved, cracks began to appear in their marriage. Both were very promiscuous and, despite their self-professed open relationship—which Angela was later to describe as a "marriage of convenience"—jealousy began to rear its head. Matters deteriorated further when Angela achieved the notable distinction of being sent home from an American tour for misconduct. Thereafter, she was forbidden from accompanying her husband on the road.

An aspiring actress, Angela auditioned for the role as television's Wonder Woman, which went to Lynda Carter. She made an appearance on *The Mike Douglas Show* in October 1975, singing the old standard "I've Got a Crush on You." The show was watched by an audience of some fourteen million viewers. After transmission, David rang to "dedicate" a new song, "Golden Years," to her. She remembered the conversation: "I think it was a coincidence because he had just finished recording the track about two hours before he saw the California airing of *The Mike Douglas Show* and he told me that the song was for me when he called right after the show to congratulate me."

The song appeared the following year on album *Station to Station*. It was offered to Elvis Presley, who shared the same record label, RCA. Angie volunteered to fly to Las Vegas, where Presley was appearing, and deliver a tape of the song personally. After witnessing Elvis's lackluster show, Angie got cold feet about meeting him and about the prospect of having to lie if asked for her views on the performance. She ended up giving the tape to one of Presley's associates; Elvis never recorded the song.

The couple divorced in 1980, after officially separating two years earlier. Bowie was granted custody of their son, Zowie Jones (now a successful BAFTA Award–winning film director). Angie has a daughter,

DAVID BOWIE originally debuted "The Prettiest Star" as a very early single before he had tasted the success that would attend his later career. Released in 1970, it failed to chart in either the U.S. or U.K. Having scored with "Space Oddity" the year before, the lack of attention "The Prettiest Star" received was quite unexpected.

It would be two years until Bowie had another U.K. hit; "Starman" reached #10 and restarted his career. "Space Oddity" topped the U.K. chart when re-released in 1975, but it wasn't until the 1980s that Bowie secured another #1 single.

Stacia, by her next long-term partner, punk musician Drew Blood. Angela now lives in Tucson, Arizona, with partner Michael Gassett. She has acted occasionally and, in 2002, released her debut album, *Moon Goddess*, which she described as a musical biography. She is working on a follow-up. Although she describes her main occupation as writing—she is the author of *The Pocket Essential Guide to Bisexuality*—Angela has occasionally worked in construction, claiming that the physical labor helps her keep weight off. She no longer has any contact with David Bowie. When asked what she would say if she were to encounter her ex-husband again, Angela replied, "I'd lie and say it was great to see him."

Angie Bowie (left) dancing with Bianca Jagger at the Ziggy Stardust farewell party, held at the Café Royal in July 1973. Only a month earlier the Stones had finished recording their single "Angie," but Mick Jagger denied it was about Bowie's wife.

MICK JAGGER vehemently denies writing the Rolling Stones' single "Angie" about Angie Bowie. "I've said about a hundred million times that it wasn't [about Angela Bowie]," wailed Jagger in 2002. "I don't think I had even met Angela Bowie when I wrote the rest of the lyrics. That was one of Keith's songs, I just filled in the gaps." Keith Richards confirms the story. "I had the whole chord sequence down maybe a year before with just the title Angie. It could have been Randy or Mangy or anything, you know, but Mick just picked up on the title and wrote a song around it."

Rikki Don't Lose That Number

Steely Dan

Bard College in Annandale-on-Hudson in New York State would play a major role in the career of Steely Dan. It was there in 1967 that Donald Fagen met Walter Becker. Fagen was strolling by a café and heard a guy practicing guitar. He thought it sounded very professional, "you know, like a black person really." They got talking and found they had the same taste in jazz music. They formed a band/songwriting partnership, though in the early days they played covers and went under the name of the Bad Rock Group and subsequently the Leather Canary.

Annandale was also the place that sparked the lyrical content for "My Old School" and "Rikki Don't Lose That Number." For many years the precise intention of the latter song was obscured, but in 2006 *Entertainment Weekly* ran a feature entitled "Back to Annandale," which revealed that it was actually written about novelist Rikki Ducornet (born Erica DeGre). In 2008 she became a writer in residence at the University of Louisiana and spoke about the circumstances in which the song was written. She was a big fan of the student band.

"At that point, Chevy Chase was the drummer—not a very good one, but he was already funny—and Donald Fagen was clearly a genius. I was actually a young faculty wife, I was pregnant, I think 2 months, and he thought I was cute. So he gave me his phone number. Which I lost. But I thought they were brilliant."

Clearly Rikki did lose that number.

After college the budding songwriters tried to sell their wares at New York's home of music publishing, the Brill Building. They managed to write a song for Barbra Streisand and became backing musicians for Jay Black's band, Jay and the Americans; yet a recording contract eluded them. Their big break came when producer Gary Katz took them to L.A. to become staff writers for ABC Records. When he realized that the songs they were writing were too complex for anyone but them, Steely Dan was born.

It took a lot longer for Ducornet to find out that they had signed a recording contract. "I didn't find out about it for 10 years. I was living in

France, and came back to Amherst, Massachusetts. I walked into a record store, and heard Fagen's voice. I recognized it at once. And I heard my name.

"Then a couple of days later, I ran into someone that I had just met, and he said, 'Hey, you know that song? Fagen wrote it for you.'"

Both Steely Dan and Ducornet have gone on to carve out substantial careers. Ducornet has produced an impressive collection of work in her time—poetry, short story

The irony of Rikki Ducornet's story is that she did lose that number, and she didn't need it anyway.

anthologies, and novels. In 2008, the American Academy of Arts and Letters gave her one of the eight annual Academy Awards presented to writers. Coincidentally her son works in the music business as a songwriter, performer, and producer—he wrote a hit song for Santana, "Hoy Es Adios."

Rikki is still not entirely sure the song that Donald Fagen wrote should be taken literally. "It's like a Zen koan to me.... What does that mean, 'Rikki don't lose that number'?"

STEELY DAN, with nine albums from 1972 to the present day, could never be described as prolific (though between 1981 and 1993 Donald Fagen and Walter Becker had gone their separate ways and pursued solo projects). Their 1972 hit singles, "Do It Again" and "Reelin' in the Years," came off debut album *Can't Buy a Thrill* and cemented their place as a mainstay of AOR (album-oriented rock) radio. But it was "Rikki Don't Lose That Number" from 1974's *Pretzel Logic* album that became their biggest U.S. hit single, reaching #4 on the Billboard chart. Their comeback album of 2000, *Two Against Nature*, was the first Steely Dan LP in twenty years and stunned Eminem by beating his *Marshal Mathers* LP to win the Grammy for Album of the Year.

Rosanna
Toto

Everyone knows that Toto's huge 1982 hit, "Rosanna," is about the actress Rosanna Arquette. It must be true: it's in all the rock encyclopedias. Everyone knows that Arquette went out with the band's guitarist, Steve Lukather, and he wrote the song for her. Like so many rock 'n' roll myths, all this is close, but no cigar.

Rosanna Arquette was a showbiz kid. Her grandfather was comedian Cliff Arquette, and her parents were both actors. She grew up in a theater in Chicago and on a commune in Virginia before hitching her way as a fifteen-year-old across the U.S. to San Francisco. Inevitably, she fell into the acting profession, making her stage debut in a musical production in Los Angeles in 1977.

Almost as inevitably, in the entertainment capital of America, she began to meet musicians. Her first marriage, in 1978, was to composer Tony Greco. It lasted barely two years—that was almost twice as long as her second marriage, in 1986, to composer James Newton Howard. Thereafter she lived with Peter Gabriel for a while (he wrote "In Your Eyes" about her) before unpredictably stepping outside the musical circle—her third marriage, which lasted six years, was to restaurateur John Sidel.

In between those first two, around 1981, she began dating a member of Toto—not initially guitarist Lukather but keyboardist Steve Porcaro—and naturally took to hanging out with the band. In 1982 they were virtually living in a recording studio, preparing their fourth album,

Rosanna Arquette was in the right place at the right time, with the right number of syllables.

Toto IV. In 1983 Arquette described how she helped out by "bringing the band juice and beer" during their all-night studio sessions.

It was not Steve Porcaro but Toto's other keyboardist and songwriter, David Paich, who wrote the song "Rosanna" and brought it to the recording sessions for the album. He says, "Rosanna is about three girls that I knew all rolled into one." It was almost complete; in fact all that was missing was the lyric for a recurring three-note musical phrase during the verses. Arquette just happened to be around dispensing juice, and her first name fit the meter of the phrase. "I think I just stole her name and stuck it on there."

There's no denying the name fits, and it's hard to imagine the song working quite so well if Steve Porcaro had been dating a Maria or a Christina or a Madonna. Peaking at #2 in the Billboard Hot 100, it was Toto's second most successful single ever and won the band a Record of the Year Grammy in 1983. David Paich tells us that Steve did write a song for Rosanna, just not this one—the ballad, "A Secret Love," from the band's second album, was composed after their first meeting, two years before they began dating.

Happily, Rosanna has returned to the musical fold since her restaurant detour. She has been linked to David Codikow, an entertainment executive best known for managing the band Velvet Revolver. Interestingly they met when he was the producer of her directorial debut, the documentary movie *Looking for Debra Winger*.

TOTO could technically be classified as a supergroup. The adult-oriented rock band comprised some of the industry's leading session musicians when it formed in 1977. They went on to release twelve studio albums in the next thirty years. "Rosanna" was the first track from the band's fourth album, *Toto IV*, released in 1982. The LP nestled in the Top 5 on both sides of the Atlantic, making it their most successful album. The single peaked at #2 in the U.S. Billboard Hot 100 but paved the way for their #1 hit, "Africa."

Though their next two albums went gold, they did not reach the Top 40—it proved to be the peak of their popularity in the U.K. and U.S. But the demand was much higher in mainland Europe and Japan, where a varying line-up continued to enjoy success, ensuring they continued to tour and release albums well into the current century.

Sara
Fleetwood Mac

It would take a whole book to document and untangle the notoriously complicated love lives of the Fleetwood Mac family. One of the great strengths of the band has been its ability to survive the innumerable affairs and fallings-out between its members, which would have torn any other band apart. Not only has it endured all that fascinating internal infidelity and romance, but the band often translated it into painfully raw, beautiful pop songs for mass entertainment.

Sara Recor with Mick Fleetwood in 1990, during their brief marriage.

Perhaps it's because they put the music first. Their 1979 hit "Sara" is a finely crafted song, but its lyrics, born of painful personal experience, are less than transparent if one looks for clues about the identity of the Sara in the title. It's been the subject of much debate and erroneous conclusion among fans and other Mac watchers.

Stevie Nicks, who wrote the song, used the pseudonym Sara Anderson when she attended the Betty Ford Clinic to deal with cocaine addiction. This episode was documented by Nicks in the song "Welcome to the Room...Sara," from the album *Tango in the Night*. Many assume that this is the same Sara—but Nicks's stay at the clinic was in 1986, seven years after the release of *Tusk*, the album on which the track was first included.

Nicks had an affair with Don Henley of the Eagles in 1977 (who was building himself a house at the time—to which there are obvious references in "Sara.") Although his paternity has never been established, she had an abortion at about the same time (to which the lyrics also make clear references). It is possible that, at least in parts of the song, Sara is the name given to her unborn child.

> And it was just like a great dark wind
> Within the wings of a storm

A year later, she was having an affair with Mick Fleetwood, the band's leader and drummer, when he—already married to Jenny Boyd and having an affair with Nicks—started a second affair, with Nicks's best friend, Sara Recor. Nicks has confirmed in interviews since that Mick was indeed the "great dark wind" of the lyric. So it seems likely that, at least in parts of the song, Sara refers to her friend. Recor eventually married Fleetwood.

Says Fleetwood Mac's Christine McVie: "Stevie's words can be pretty obscure at best. In her mind, her words make complete sense and I often used to wonder what on earth she was talking about." The original unreleased recording of the song, edited down to seven minutes for the album and four for the single, ran to an epic sixteen minutes. It included nine more verses that were never made public, reputedly about other members of the band. So much has been left out that there's little wonder some of the sense of the words may have been lost.

Stevie Nicks has hinted at all three possible identities, and in 1994, she said, "She [Sara Recor] likes to think it's completely about her, but it's really not completely about her. It's about me, about her, about Mick, about Fleetwood Mac. It's about all of us at that point."

FLEETWOOD MAC has always been a fluid entity; yet it has managed to maintain success for a prolonged period from the 1960s to the 1990s. Frequent changes in members and musical direction have helped the Anglo-American band remain popular throughout the years. "Sara" was released on *Tusk*, their expensively produced third album, with Stevie Nicks as vocalist. Their previous two LPs had represented an upturn in the band's fortunes, both hitting the top spot on the Billboard chart. *Tusk* didn't equal this but still reached #4. Follow-up album *Mirage* again topped the U.S. charts, and they continued to release albums into the twenty-first century and started touring again, despite many more alterations in personnel. It seems the popularity of Fleetwood Mac endures, regardless of who is holding the instruments.

See Emily Play
Pink Floyd

Pink Floyd was trying to make an impression on the swinging London scene of 1966 when an encounter between an ingénue schoolgirl and songwriter Syd Barrett became the lyrical inspiration for their most important hit. In the original line-up of the band, art student Syd Barrett was the talismanic lead singer-guitarist, along with architecture students Roger Waters (bass), Rick Wright (keyboards), and Nick Mason (drums).

Emily Young in a passport photo from the 1960s.

Not yet signed to a record label, the Pink Floyd Sound, as they were known, started a residency at All Saints Hall, just off Ladbroke Grove in West London. The band was heavily into psychedelia, sometimes combining forty-minute extended tracks with an innovative light show and Barrett's talent for word association and vivid imagery. In the early days of the residency, few came to share the psychedelic vision, but gradually the buzz and the audience built. Emily Young, daughter of the Labour politician Wayland Hilton Young—the 2nd Baron Kennet—was a pupil at the trendy Holland Park School nearby. She was also best friends with Anjelica Huston, daughter of film director John Huston. The fifteen-year-old Emily had various reported nicknames at the time, including "Far Out Em" and "The Psychedelic Schoolgirl." After a gig at All Saints they came back to one of the Floyd managers' houses nearby and shared a joint with Barrett and the band.

The Beatles' record label, EMI, signed the band in January and their debut single, "Arnold Layne," was a success. They needed a follow-up, so Syd changed the lyrics to a song he'd written for the notorious Games for May concert at the Festival Hall (where a bubble machine had left ring marks on the plush seats). The song was "See Emily Play." Around this time, friends and his fellow band members started to see an ominous deterioration in Syd's mental health, but he still had his playful side. In one of his characteristic meanders, Syd told a journalist that he'd "seen Emily dancing naked in a wood, when he'd slept under the stars after a gig up north."

The single reached #5 in the U.K. charts in 1967 and propelled Pink Floyd firmly into the mainstream; yet Emily was oblivious to the fact that the song was written about her.

"My friend and I used to go dancing on a Friday night, and the band was this thing called The Pink Floyd Sound." She told the *Times* in 2001. "I didn't pay that much attention to them because I was sort of dancing around and chatting—there was a bunch of crazy people in Notting Hill in those days, lots of poets and beatnik types. Somebody wrote a biography of Syd Barrett the other day and they said that I was a fan and that's why I was there. And I have to say that I really wasn't—I barely paid attention to the band because I was far more interested in these beat poets."

After traveling the world and studying at Chelsea and St. Martin's art schools, she lived and worked with Simon Jeffes in the 1970s and '80s. Jeffes was the creative inspiration behind the Penguin Cafe Orchestra, an experimental classical ensemble whose quirky, innovative music incorporated little-used instruments such as ukeles and harmoniums. They produced music that would be used to augment a host of TV programs and advertising campaigns. Like Barrett's Pink Floyd, they also gigged at the Festival Hall. Emily produced the surrealist artwork for the albums.

Art ran in the family. Her grandmother, Kathleen Scott, was a pupil of Auguste Rodin and the widow of the famous explorer Robert Falcon Scott (of the Antarctic). So it was perhaps no surprise that she should take up sculpture almost by accident, when she found stone carving tools left behind in her house by workers after a renovation project. Through the late 1990s and into the twenty-first century, she has established herself as Britain's most influential female sculptor, taking over the mantle of Elizabeth Frink and Barbara Hepworth.

The free spirit that Syd Barrett found so (fleetingly) attractive lives on. "The '60s was a very interesting time, all sorts of ideas were becoming popular that are now being borne out one hundred percent," she told the BBC's Felicity Finch. "The kind of stuff that people sneered at. But the kind of mess the world is in at the moment requires that visionary optimistic thinking. We sensed it back then when we were young."

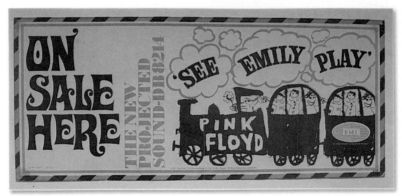

A promotional poster destined for record shop windows across the U.K. in 1967. Lead singer and former art student Syd Barrett created the artwork.

Emily creates many different pieces but is perhaps most famous for carving angels, and her divine messengers are installed around St. Paul's Cathedral in London and Salisbury Cathedral in Wiltshire. She has also produced a work entitled "Howl," which has echoes of the Pink Floyd track "Scream Thy Last Scream," and a famous artwork of a screaming face (produced by Syd himself in the 1960s).

Sculpting hasn't come without physical pain. After an accident in the studio she needed restorative surgery to sew back her thumb and part of her hand but insists that "neurosurgery these days is fantastic."

The subjects for her sculptures often suggest themselves. "I sort of anthropomorphise with each piece of stone—what I think it wants to be worked [into]. I think they're quite interested to be turned into sculptures. You never know what you're going to find inside a piece of stone but sometimes you get wonderful things happening and the figuration of the stone follows the contours you're aiming at."

Today she works out of a studio in West London, only a short distance from the place where she first heard Pink Floyd perform in the mid-sixties. She's happy to listen to "See Emily Play," "which I carry on playing in my studio with my stones." But she is gently insistent that she is not, to quote the lyric, "the girl who tries but misunderstands."

"He really didn't know me well enough to form any opinion about my character; he saw me, that really is all. The song is most definitely a conversation between the original Syd and the drug-damaged person he was turning into. I was his representation to himself of his own mad muse, the new Syd, who was losing touch with reality, and making

One of Young's impressive sculptures, **Wounded Angel,** *during its time in Kew Gardens.*

mistakes, thinking he was playing, but misunderstanding. The poetic muse often takes a feminine form. It was him who was crying, him who sailed forever on the river ... it seems so obvious once one thinks of it that way. So it's a compliment to me to have been chosen as the embodiment of his magical talent, but it's really not about me at all."

PINK FLOYD was a group that evolved with the times, moving from 1960s psychedelia to a more progressive rock sound in the 1970s and 1980s. "See Emily Play" was only their second single release and a fine example of Syd Barrett–inspired pop whimsey. It reached #6 in the U.K. but failed to crack the Top 100 in the U.S.; that landmark would have to wait until "Money" reached #13 in 1973. The album from which it was taken, *Dark Side of the Moon,* included themes of mental illness; critics have often remarked that Floyd's best songs—"Shine On You Crazy Diamond" and "Wish You Were Here"—were written about Barrett out of remorse for dumping their founder member. Bassist Roger Waters left after his working relationship with singer-guitarist David Gilmour (who replaced Syd) floundered. The band reunited for Bob Geldof's Live 8 in 2005, but further concerts are not expected.

She's Leaving Home
The Beatles

Melanie Coe's mother was shocked when she found the note that would ultimately inspire a Beatles song. She worked as a hairdresser in London's East End and counted the mother of gangland bosses Ronnie and Reggie Kray among her clients. One evening she came home to find the "I'm leaving home" note that her seventeen-year-old daughter had written.

Surprisingly, the story of a teenager running away made the front page of the *Daily Mirror*. Reading the story, Paul McCartney began to write "She's Leaving Home," never imagining for a second that he had met Melanie Coe three years previously.

When the Beatles first burst on the pop scene, the number-one U.K. pop program was *Ready Steady Go!* and Paul had to judge a competition for presenter Brian Mathew.

"I first met Paul when I was 13 on *Ready Steady Go!* He presented me with first prize for miming to Brenda Lee's 'Let's Jump the Broomstick,' which meant I danced on the show for a year." Competing against three other girls, Melanie danced and mimed her way through the number (the clip can still be seen on YouTube). It was a big moment for the wide-eyed teenager.

Melanie Coe, twenty-five years after the release of **Sgt. Pepper.**

"We had spent a long day in the studio filming. John Lennon was aloof and unapproachable, Paul shook our hands but Ringo and George were sweethearts, chatting to us all day."

By the time she was seventeen her parents had seemingly spoiled her with diamonds and furs, and she had her very own car—highly unusual for a British teenager of the 1960s. But then she got pregnant and feared the consequences if she told her mother.

In real life she left in the afternoon when she knew her parents would be out, but instead of meeting "a man in the motor trade" she ran off with a croupier. They stayed in Bayswater in west London and managed to evade her parents for ten days before they were discovered. She had made the mistake of telling her parents where her boyfriend worked. Back home in suburban Stamford Hill she was obliged to have an abortion. "As a 17-year-old I had everything money could buy—but my father and mother never once told me they loved me," Melanie has said.

Within a year she managed to leave home less controversially when she married a Spaniard, celebrating with a lavish reception at the Dorchester hotel in London. The newlyweds moved to the Bahamas, but the marriage lasted only a year. When it ended, Melanie headed for Los Angeles, intent on an acting career. She dated Burt Ward, who played Robin in the *Batman* TV series, but the big break never came. She returned from America in 1981 to look after her mother.

In 1997 she left home from Snape in rural Suffolk and moved to Tarifa in southern Spain. But her dream move turned into a nightmare when she was forced to demolish a $200,000 property that the local authorities declared had been built illegally on National Park land. "I've always lived life to the hilt. I have never played safe," says Melanie. "But having to demolish my house is the most stressful thing I've ever known."

THE BEATLES were not one of the 1960s bands that were not permitted to play on their own records, but "She's Leaving Home," (yet another track from their 1967 masterpiece *Sgt. Pepper's Lonely Hearts Club Band*), saw them star in a vocal role only. Writer Paul McCartney had wanted George Martin to write an orchestral arrangement for the song, but he was too busy and asked Mike Leander to do it. The musicians involved included Sheila Bromberg on harp, the first woman to be specially engaged to play on a Beatles track. Though not directly involved, George Martin later confessed the result had moved him to tears. "She's Leaving Home" also appeared on the compilations *Love Songs* and *The Beatles Ballads*.

Something / Layla
George Harrison and Eric Clapton

There must have been something about Pattie Boyd. When the London model was cast as a schoolgirl in the first Beatles film, she was asked out by George Harrison and turned him down. The "shy one" of the Beatles wasn't put off, though.

The year was 1964. Beatlemania had taken hold in the U.K. and had just exploded in the U.S. Boyd wasn't a Beatles fan and almost backed out of her first film job—she was more used to high profile fashion work with the likes of top London photographer David Bailey, and she was worried she would embarrass herself in an acting role. But her agent insisted she turn up for the part of a schoolgirl in what would turn out to be *A Hard Day's Night*.

She played the part of one of four schoolgirls who cornered the Beatles after they escaped from fans onto a train. The film company had chartered a train for the day, which

The photo session that started rock's most famous love triangle.

took them from London to Cornwall and back, giving them quite a bit of time together. As they were approaching London, George asked her to marry him, or, at least, come out for dinner. Unsure of just how serious he was, she turned him down. She had a boyfriend.

On her way home she immediately regretted what she'd said, as she was in a relationship with an older man that had all but run its course.

And her friends couldn't believe she'd turned down a Beatle. Luckily she saw George again for a press photo-op at Twickenham studios, where each of the four girls from the train had to tousle a Beatle's hair. She made a beeline for Harrison, and when George asked her out again he got a different answer. Their first date was at the Garrick Club in Covent Garden, and Beatles manager Brian Epstein came along too. Five days later, on Pattie's twentieth birthday, March 17, 1964, she took George home to see her mother and father. They were an item.

Pattie Boyd married George Harrison in January 1966 at Epsom Registry Office, and they left for their honeymoon in Barbados. In her autobiography, *Wonderful Today*, Pattie describes how she first heard about "Something." George played it for her in the kitchen of their house in Esher. "He told me in a matter-of-fact way, that he had written it for me. I thought it was beautiful and it turned out to be the most successful song he ever wrote."

With enough material already written for the album *The Beatles*, it would eventually see the light of day on *Abbey Road*. Though by 1996, having remarried Olivia Arias, Harrison saw the song in a different light. "I just wrote it, and then somebody put together a video. And what they did was they went out and got some footage of me and Pattie, Paul and Linda, Ringo and Maureen. So then, everybody presumed I wrote it about Pattie, but actually, when I wrote it, I was thinking of Ray Charles."

By 1970 the Beatles had split up acrimoniously, and Pattie and George had moved to Friar Park in Henley-on-Thames, a grand gothic house set in thirty-six acres to which George invited all, including many from the Hare Krishna movement.

Eric Clapton and George had become friends in the late 1960s. The pair had written the song "Badge" together, which Eric performed in supergroup Cream. Eric had been a previous visitor to the Harrison's house in Esher and had started dating Pattie's younger, wilder sister Paula. Harrison became preoccupied with his solo career, his spiritual life, and with restoring the garden at Friar Park, all of which left Pattie feeling neglected. She began to enjoy the flirtation of random secret meetings with Clapton through the spring and summer of 1970, confessing that "the convent girl in me found the situation uncomfortable but at the same time strangely exciting."

Then one afternoon Eric took her to a flat in South Kensington and played her a track he'd recorded with his band, the Dominos, in Miami. "Layla" was based on the book by Persian writer Nezami, entitled *Layla and Majnun*, about a man who falls in love with a woman who loves him

Boyd's modeling career dwindled in the mid-1960s, as George Harrison preferred her to stay home.

but is not free. Boyd was thrilled but worried as she recalls in her autobiography: "My first thought was 'Oh God, everyone's going to know who this is.'" Later that day they met up at a party at Robert Stigwood's house in North London, and when George arrived later on, to her horror Eric confessed to his friend that he was in love with his wife. The Harrisons went home and Pattie threw herself into work at Friar Park, while Clapton turned to heroin and a relationship with Alice Ormsby-Gore.

But relations between Harrison and Clapton hadn't been ended by his confession of love. In August 1971, when George organized the Concert for Bangladesh in New York, a worse-for-wear Clapton flew in to play. Back home Pete Townshend helped Eric get treatment for his addictions, and in his recovery phase Clapton became a regular visitor at Friar Park. He had not given up his romantic pursuit, though, and each time Boyd gently sidestepped the situation. But in 1973 Pattie discovered that George was having serious flings, first with Ronnie Wood's wife, Krissie, and then with Ringo's wife, Maureen Starkey—these discoveries finally proved to be the catalysts for change.

Feeling isolated and undervalued, in July she made the final decision to leave George and join her sister Jenny and Mick Fleetwood in L.A. She'd been there a week when Eric got in touch. He was touring his *461 Ocean Boulevard* album across America. Eight days later they met up in Boston and Boyd joined him on his twenty-six-date tour. It was only then she realized that Clapton had ditched the heroin and replaced it with alcohol.

Boyd's defection to Clapton hadn't ended the musicians' relationship, though. That Christmas Harrison joined them both at Clapton's house in Surrey on Christmas Day, where the only point of contention was that Pattie had given up the vegetarianism she had maintained for so many years while living with George. Eric and George began to refer to themselves jokingly as "husbands-in-law."

After a world tour kept them out of the country for a year in 1975, they settled back down to a heavy-drinking lifestyle in their upper-class home. Eric was going through different musical phases, and the simplicity of Don Williams's country style appealed. One evening Pattie was getting ready, putting dresses on, taking dresses off, while Eric was strumming at the guitar downstairs: "When I finally got downstairs and asked the inevitable question, 'Do I look all right?' he played me what he'd written." The result was "Wonderful Tonight," which made it a trio of classic love songs.

However, it wasn't long before Eric's song "The Shape You're In" became a more accurate reflection of their time together. Eric sang, "Well my little girl really loves that wine / Wine will do it for her most every time." The drinking, infidelity, and rock 'n' roll lifestyle was wearing them down, accentuated by the fact that Pattie couldn't have children and at thirty-six was considered too old to adopt.

Eric with Pattie in January 1975, just before setting out on a year-long tour.

She left Clapton in 1984 and was almost persuaded back, but then she discovered Eric had fathered a child, Conor, with an Italian woman Lori del Santo. Even so, the couple persisted, unsuccessfully, with in vitro fertilization treatment, and Clapton started commuting to Milan in January 1987 in order to see his son. Finally, as a result of one drunken argument too many, Boyd packed her bags and left. Clapton checked into rehab and they were divorced by 1989.

Tragedy would strike Clapton in 1991 when his son fell to his death in New York through a fifty-third-floor window a cleaner had left open. Both Pattie and George Harrison attended the funeral in Surrey.

Since her divorce Boyd and Clapton have remained friends, and when Harrison died from cancer in 2001, Eric helped organize the memorial concert. It was an improbably amicable love triangle. Boyd regrets having not fought harder to save her marriage to her "soulmate" George, but she is proud to have been the inspiration for three classic love songs.

Suite: Judy Blue Eyes
By Crosby, Stills & Nash

The song cycle "Suite: Judy Blue Eyes" holds a resonant place in folk-rock history. It was the first track on the phenomenally successful first LP by Crosby, Stills & Nash, the supergroup summit of the 1960s folk-rock movement. It was the song that opened their set at Woodstock in 1969 and closed their set in Philadelphia for Live Aid in 1985. And it was the song that chronicled the breakup of Stephen Stills's relationship with singer Judy Collins, a leading light and already a veteran of the U.S. folk revival.

Collins was five years Stills's senior, beautiful, and possessed of piercing blue eyes. In 1967 when she and Stephen first became an item, she had just released *Wildflowers*, her seventh LP in as many years and her first gold album. She had begun to introduce new elements to her repertoire—songs from musical theater, and from new, little-known contemporary folk artists such as Joni Mitchell (a Grammy-winning version of whose song "Both Sides Now" she included on *Wildflowers*) and Leonard Cohen (whose song "Suzanne" she recorded in 1966, a year before he did).

Collins was already breaking musical boundaries, and now so was everyone else. It was the Summer of Love, and nowhere more so than in California. Around one hundred thousand hippies descended on Haight Ashbury in San Francisco, and their soundtrack was the genre-blending folk- and country-rock of Buffalo Springfield and the Byrds.

Stills was guitarist and songwriter with the Springfield and appeared on Collins's next LP, *Who Knows Where the Time Goes*, in 1968. When the group disbanded that year in the face of bitter musical differences, he began jamming and writing new material with David Crosby (a former lover of Joni Mitchell), who had been fired by his group, the Byrds, the previous year, after their performance at the Monterey Pop Festival.

In the summer of 1968, at the home of Cass Elliot, in the bohemian Los Angeles neighborhood of Laurel Canyon, Judy Collins was rehearsing with her band. At a party in Joni Mitchell's apartment across the canyon, Stills and Crosby were trying out new songs they had been working on. Suddenly another guest, Graham Nash, himself falling head over heals in love with Joni Mitchell, unexpectedly joined in with a third harmony. The blend of those three voices for the first time was electric and the room fell silent, awestruck. Crosby and Stills had been looking for a third member of their new band; that night, at that party, Crosby, Stills & Nash was born.

Echoing Buffalo Springfield's disintegration since the Summer of Love, Stills and Collins's love affair was also collapsing under tension. Both were

Judy Collins is better known for performing other people's songs than her own, but she's also responsible for inspiring an eight-minute Woodstock classic.

at the top of their respective games, very much in the public eye, very much under pressure to deliver strong new material—the relationship was bound to suffer. Stills expressed his distress in lyric form.

> Tearing yourself away from me now
> You are free and I am crying
> This does not mean I don't love you
> I do, that's forever

"It poured out of me over many months," he says, "and filled several notebooks. I had a hell of a time getting the music to fit." Faced with several fragments of songs half begun from his outpourings, he decided to join them together in a song cycle, a suite of songs.

He refined the arrangement and eventually went with his guitar to the hotel where blue-eyed Judy was staying for a concert she was giving in California. He played the suite to her in its entirety. Recalling that first hearing, Collins says, "It was supposed to get me back. I thought it was beautiful, so beautiful—and too bad it's not going to work."

She was present in the studio when he recorded several demos, including "Suite: Judy Blue Eyes," late in 1968; Stills remembers her telling him not to work all night. But the following year she left Stills for the actor Stacy Keach, whom she had met while appearing in a production of *Peer Gynt* in New York.

On the version of the song recorded for the first Crosby, Stills & Nash album, those electric vocal harmonies are in place, delivered by all three singers. But Stephen Stills plays all the instruments himself, as if the song and the heartbreak it describes were too personal to entrust to anyone else.

The result is seven and a half minutes of exquisite music, described by the critic Jason Ankeny as "an epic love song, remarkable in its musical and emotional intricacy." Its changing rhythms, jangling acoustic guitars, and close, soaring vocals seem to embody the heady optimism of those years when all things were possible. Only the lyrics spell out Stephen Stills's desperate, underlying sadness.

In 1971, when *Rolling Stone* noted that Collins was still the subject of much of Stills's songwriting output, Stephen replied, "Well, there are three things men can do with women: love them, suffer for them, or turn them into literature. I've had my share of success and failure at all three."

Judy Collins remains an unassailable cultural icon to this day. She is a singer with some forty albums to her credit; she is an author of memoirs and novels; and she has carried the flag of liberal protest throughout her life. In 1969 she testified at the trial of anti-Vietnam demonstrators by singing the song "Where Have All the Flowers Gone?" Times may change, but she, it seems, does not: in 1995 she was appointed a Goodwill Ambassador for UNICEF, for which she now campaigns energetically for the outlawing of landmines.

It was at a fundraising event in 1978 for the Equal Rights Amendment that she met Louis Nelson, a graphic designer and fellow campaigner, whom she would eventually marry in 1996 and for whom she wrote "Wedding Song (Song for Louis)."

She and Stills remain on good terms, however. At a dinner with her and her granddaughter a couple years ago, Stephen remarked that he was sorry Judy had never earned any royalties from the song for which she had been such an inspiration. Judy's granddaughter quickly joked, "Well, it's never too late."

Of the song which immortalized so publicly such an exciting but painful period in the lives of both Stills and Collins, Judy says, "He wove all that together in this magnificent creation. So the legacy of our relationship is certainly in that song."

CROSBY, STILLS & NASH were a supergroup formed from members of the Byrds, Buffalo Springfield, and the Hollies respectively. They released "Suite: Judy Blue Eyes" on their self-titled debut LP in 1969, where it reached #21 in the U.S.; it was a precursor for the success the group would have in the coming years.

They went on to have six Top 10 albums and significant critical acclaim for their vocal harmonies, despite turbulent relationships between them (amplified by the addition of Stills's former Buffalo Springfield bandmate Neil Young).

Splits and partial reformations peppered their career, but they continue to tour today as a trio. All four band members have been inducted to the Rock and Roll Hall of Fame twice—for their work with CSN&Y and their respective bands. It is a testament to their impact on music.

Suzanne
Leonard Cohen

Suzanne Verdal first met Leonard Cohen in the early 1960s when she was still a teenager. They met at Le Vieux Moulin jazz club in Montreal, where she danced with her lover and soon-to-be-husband, sculptor Armand Villaincourt. "The Beat scene was beautiful, we were just dancing our hearts out for hours on end, happy on very little," recalls Verdal.

Cohen would watch her dance, aware perhaps that he was a lot older than most of those on the scene—he was in his late twenties and had a growing reputation as a poet and author—and that Suzanne was the muse of many of Montreal's aspiring beat poets. When Suzanne and Armand endured a painful separation, she went to live with their daughter Julie in a house down by the St. Lawrence River, and in the summer of 1965, Cohen became a regular visitor.

"Leonard heard about this place I was living, with crooked floors and a poetic view of the river, and he came to visit me many times. We had tea together many times and mandarin oranges."

Though Verdal was flattered by the attention, the encounters took on a bohemian, almost spiritual quality. Long before Cohen would retreat from the world into the Mount Baldy Zen Buddhist Monastery, he was sitting down for tea ceremonies with Suzanne Verdal.

Verdal recalled, "I would always light a candle and serve tea and it would be quiet for several minutes. Then we would speak. And I would speak about life and poetry and we'd share ideas."

Though Cohen was clearly smitten with Suzanne, there was only a meeting of minds, not bodies; the passion the poet felt went unrequited, as the song alludes:

> And you want to travel blind
> And you know that she will trust you
> For you've touched her perfect body
> With your mind

"Suzanne Brings You Down" first appeared in a collection of poems published in 1966, entitled *Parasites of Heaven*. But if it had been intended as a love letter that exposed the depth of emotion felt by a tormented soul, then it missed its target. Verdal left her place by the river and went traveling with her daughter, and it wasn't till she returned that a mutual friend told her, "Did you hear the wonderful poem Leonard wrote for you?"

The Notre-Dame-de-Bon-Secours Chapel in Montreal, known as the Sailors' Chapel.

Luckily for Cohen's career, Judy Collins heard it too, urged the poet to set it to music, and then recorded it herself. On the back of the song's success Cohen was able to get a record deal and establish himself, through the late 1960s and early 1970s, as the "thinking woman's favorite." It would also lead to the anthemic "Hallelujah," one of the most covered songs in music history.

Thus Suzanne Verdal's part in Leonard Cohen's career is very significant. The poem/song is not a flight of fantasy but a portrait of her lifestyle. She was the woman living by the river, feeding him tea and oranges, "wearing rags and feathers from Salvation Army counters." She took him for walks along the river, where they would pass the Notre-Dame-de-Bon-Secours Chapel, with its image of Jesus as a sailor. So how does she feel about her story launching his career?

"Flattered somewhat. But I was depicted as I think, in sad terms too in a sense, and that's a little unfortunate. You know I don't think I was quite as sad as that—though maybe I was and he perceived that and I didn't. Poets, when they have a vision or an image, of course, use that. What came later was not remaining friends with Leonard and not knowing why. And that's why there was some ill feeling there or some sadness that was not there at the beginning at all. Now the words have more meaning in a sense, because there's a kind of detachment in the song that I hear now, that I didn't hear then."

The story of Suzanne doesn't just end with Cohen leaving town for a career in the music business and the players in the drama becoming estranged. Having pioneered the habits of recycling and patching clothes from the early sixties, Verdal continued her hippie lifestyle in the 1970s and 1980s. She found work as a dancer, choreographer, and massage therapist. When Cohen emerged as a successful recording artist, there were subsequent encounters over the years that added intriguing footnotes to the unrequited love story.

"Once, when he was visiting Montreal, I saw him briefly in a hotel and it was a very, very wonderful happy moment because he was on his way to becoming the great success he is. And the moment arose that we

LEONARD COHEN has one of the most unusual careers in music history. Born in Montreal in 1934, he found fame as a poet and author in Canada before turning his attention to music. When he first touted his songs around New York in 1966 at the age of thirty-two, agents said, "Aren't you a little old for this game?"

The poem "Suzanne Takes You Down" first appeared in his poetry book, *Parasites of Heaven,* in 1966 and, like many of his poems, was adapted into a song. His big break came when Judy Collins agreed to cover the song in 1966, after Cohen sang it on the phone to her. "Suzanne" was the first song on his debut album of 1967, *The Songs of Leonard Cohen,* and—along with "Hallelujah" (one of the most frequently re-recorded songs of all time) and "Bird on a Wire"—is one of his most recognized works. Since

emerging from his 1990s Buddhist retreat, he has recorded with U2 and conquered the depression that has often threatened to overwhelm him throughout his career. Ironically, like Suzanne Verdal, Cohen experienced crippling money woes after he accused his longtime manager (and former lover), Kelley Lynch, of stealing more than five million dollars in retirement savings, reportedly leaving him with only $150,000.

could have a moment together intimately, and I declined."

Over subsequent years, there were encounters remembered and forgotten. In Minneapolis she went backstage "and he received me very beautifully, 'Oh Suzanne, you gave me a beautiful song.' And it was a sweet moment."

But since then it has not been so sweet. In the 1980s Suzanne was dancing on the street, busking in Montreal's popular Place Jacques Cartier. "Leonard Cohen came up to me. I saw him in the crowd and I went up to him and I curtsied to him, and after the dance was done, he walked away. I didn't understand. There was no acknowledgment from Leonard, and I did think about that for quite a while, actually. It was rather upsetting.

Cohen's first performance of "Suzanne" was with Judy Collins onstage in Central Park, July 1967.

"I stayed true to art for art's sake but he moved on. I stayed true to the cause, as it were. I don't know if that intimidated him, embarrassed him or made him uncomfortable."

In 1992 Suzanne Verdal left Montreal to move to Santa Monica. Her son Kahlil helped her build a wooden gypsy caravan on the back of a truck, out of which she has lived ever since. An accident in 1999 left her with painful multiple fractures, and she finds it almost impossible to continue to work as a choreographer or masseuse. There is a Friends of Suzanne Web site that was set up to try and help her into permanent accommodation, which, at the time of writing, has fallen into inactivity. The restless hand-to-mouth existence that Leonard Cohen found so attractive in the early sixties has never left her.

Sweet Caroline
Neil Diamond

Neil Diamond always wanted to be a singer, but his notable early successes were as a songwriter rather than as a performer. In the mid-1960s several of his catchy pop songs were covered by a wide range of artists, from Deep Purple ("Kentucky Woman") to the Monkees ("I'm a Believer" and others). Their ability to become hits in many genres demonstrated the strength of his songwriting talent, which, in turn, drew attention to him as a performer. After a dip in his fortunes toward the end of the decade, it was the song "Sweet Caroline" that relaunched his career and began to earn him a reputation for more reflective, personal songwriting.

The song was inspired, Diamond revealed in 2007, by a photograph on a 1962 cover of *Life* magazine. The caption read "On Her Pony Macaroni." It showed a young girl in a smart riding outfit cantering around a paddock. She was pretty and carefree but concentrating with all the serious focus of a determined five-year-old. "It was such an innocent, wonderful picture, I immediately felt there was a song in there." It was a picture of President John F. Kennedy's daughter, the young Caroline Kennedy.

He tucked the idea away, as songwriters do, for later use. By 1969 he was in the midst of a divorce from his first wife, by whom he had two young daughters of his own. Perhaps the painful disintegration of his family is why he returned one day to the memory of that innocent image. Sitting in a hotel room in Memphis, he spent only about an hour writing both music and lyrics of the classic hit.

It took him rather longer to admit to the public, and indeed to the woman herself, that Caroline Kennedy had been its inspiration. He had always felt that, when he did reveal Sweet Caroline's identity, she should be the first to know. "I thought maybe I would tell it to Caroline when I met her someday." He finally did so in 2007, on the occasion of her fiftieth birthday. "I'm happy to have gotten it off my chest and to have expressed it to Caroline," he said afterwards. "I thought she might be embarrassed, but she seemed to be struck by it and really, really happy."

The news that this hugely popular song was inspired by her image must have been a strangely public tribute for Caroline. She has led as private a life as is possible, considering her father was JFK. A year after that photograph was printed again, with the headline "The Fun of Being Caroline Kennedy," and just a week before her sixth birthday, her father was assassinated.

Although as a nine-year-old she was allowed to launch the aircraft carrier *USS John F. Kennedy*, the rest of her childhood was largely shielded from public gaze. She has conducted her adult life very much as a private citizen, making the protection of her personal life, her marriage, and her

Caroline with her mother, Jaqueline Kennedy, enjoying a ski vacation in Sun Valley, Idaho, April 1966.

children a priority. She studied journalism and later law, and in the 1990s she coauthored two well-regarded books on civil liberties and the right to privacy.

She serves on the board of several nonprofit organizations, with a particular interest in the funding and provision of public schools. In addition she has borne the full weight, with the death of her brother John in 1999, of the Kennedy legacy; she represents the family at presidential occasions such as funerals and memorial dedications.

She has tended to avoid direct involvement in politics, despite the constant expectation of involvement for any member of the Kennedy clan. However, in January 2008 she entered the fray in the most powerful way imaginable—with a ringing endorsement of Barack Obama. She declared, "I have never had a president who inspired me the way people tell me that my father inspired them. But for the first time, I believe I have found the man who could be that president." There followed calls for her to fill the Senate seat vacated by Hillary Clinton when she was appointed Secretary of State. Although she happily campaigned for Obama, Caroline continues to decline public office.

In disclosing Sweet Caroline's identity after nearly forty years, Neil Diamond acknowledged his debt of gratitude to the young girl whose innocence drove the song's creation: "It was a Number 1 record and probably is the biggest, most important song of my career, and I have to thank her for the inspiration."

NEIL DIAMOND's "Sweet Caroline" became his first U.S. Top 5 hit in 1969. As a songwriter he had been there before, writing "I'm a Believer" and "A Little Bit Me, A Little Bit You" for the Monkees. Songs like "Cracklin' Rosie" and "Song Sung Blue" would just be two of his hits in the next two decades, a total of thirty-seven Top 40 singles by 2009.

Diamond continues to perform and finally scored his first U.S. #1 album in 2008 with *Home Before* *Dark*, more than four decades after his debut LP.

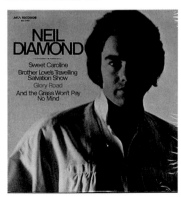

Sweet Child o' Mine
Guns N' Roses

Young lovers Erin Everly and William Rose, better known to millions as Axl, met in 1986 in a flurry of passion, embarking on a tumultuous relationship that would eventually threaten to destroy them both.

Daughter of Don, one half of long-running U.S. pop duo the Everly Brothers, Erin was no stranger to celebrity; indeed her mother, Venetia Stevenson, was also accustomed to the limelight in her career as an actress. So it was fitting that Erin met Axl while working as a model in Hollywood, where his band were beginning to make waves on the local music scene.

It is said they met when Everly attended a live show. Rose's infatuation with her was apparent immediately, and it manifested itself in the early part of their relationship as an unfinished poem about her. This formed the basis for what would become one of the most successful and recognizable rock 'n' roll songs in history.

After guitarist Slash played the introductory riff at a jam session and rhythm guitarist Izzy Stradlin joined in, Rose was so taken by the hook he wasted no time in applying it to his ode to Erin. A smash hit was forged in less than half an hour.

But the process that created the anthemic love song began as a joke, as Slash told a magazine in 1992. "I was sitting around making funny faces acting like an idiot and played that riff. Izzy started playing the chords that I was playing, strumming them, and all of a sudden Axl really liked it."

He went on to reveal his initial contempt for the song, which stemmed from a guitar riff rather than subject matter. "I hated the guitar part. Now I really like it because I've gotten it to the point where it sounds really good when I play it live. But it definitely wasn't something I hummed out in my head."

Rose corroborated the story: "I had written this poem, reached a dead end with it and put it on the shelf. Then Slash and Izzy got working together on songs and I came in. It just all came together. A lot of rock bands are too fucking wimpy to have any sentiment or any emotion in any of their stuff unless they're in pain. It's the first positive love song

Erin Everly and Axl Rose pose for a studio session in 1990. They were married at Cupid's Inn Las Vegas, the same year after he gave her an ultimatum.

I've ever written, but I never had anyone to write anything about before, I guess."

Certainly the lyrics were reflective of a man completely infatuated with a muse. The song proved the band's passport to superstardom when it became a hit in the summer of 1988, and its video enjoyed heavy rotation on MTV. It helped send its parent album, *Appetite for Destruction*, to the top of the Billboard listings a full fifty weeks after its 1987 release; by the following February, sales had surpassed quintuple platinum. But the reality soon became strikingly different for the lovers.

Everly left Rose in 1991 and relocated to Atlanta. She is now a mother of three.

When the song was released it had seemed like the romance was firmly on track, but behind the scenes was a fiery union heading for meltdown, quite contrary to the lyric, "She's got eyes of the bluest skies / I hate to look into those eyes and see an ounce of pain."

There were reports of Rose physically assaulting Everly on a regular basis, and acquaintances even claimed to have witnessed it in public. But Everly stood by her man, attributing his behavior to his well-publicized traumatic childhood. She later told *People* magazine: "I always believed things would get better, and I felt sorry for him. I thought I could make [his early childhood suffering] all better."

It was characteristic of their relationship that, after moving out of their home, Rose confronted Everly in 1990 and reportedly offered an ultimatum: "Marry me or I'll shoot myself." The gun in his car was enough incentive for the couple to head to Las Vegas, amidst Rose's promises of an abuse-free life together.

It was not to be, and, after Rose reverted to his old ways, Everly suffered a miscarriage. She then decided enough was enough. "I'd lost everything; I had no more fight and no more compassion for the abuse he had gone through."

The marriage was annulled in early 1991, and Axl reflected with regret on the chaotic relationship: "It really breaks me down to tears a lot of times when I think about how terribly we've treated each other. Erin and I treated each other like shit. Sometimes we treated each other great, because the children in us were best friends. But then there were other times when we just fucked each other's lives completely up." In a revealing interview in *Rolling Stone* in 1992, Axl claimed that rejection from his mother and his grandmother's negative feelings toward men gave him a problem relating to the opposite sex. "I've been hell on the women in my life and the women in my life have been hell on me," he admitted, adding, "but I love women."

Rose went on to date another model, Stephanie Seymour, between 1991 and 1993, continuing to make music with Guns N' Roses until they dropped out of the limelight amidst in-house fights and dissent and resulting line-up changes. He assembled a new GN'R line-up and released the band's eagerly awaited comeback album, *Chinese Democracy*, in 2008 to mixed reviews.

Everly stopped modeling and eventually married Atlanta architect Jack Portman in 1997, three years after filing a civil lawsuit against Rose for the abuse she suffered; Rose eventually settled out of court. It was illustrative of the rocky ride the pair endured in their five-year romance. But for the length of one song at least, good things were displayed for all to see—a beacon of light in an otherwise dark union.

GUNS N' ROSES is one of the most notorious rock bands in America, despite numerous line-up changes and a long period of inactivity. "Sweet Child o' Mine" was the group's second single from their debut album, *Appetite for Destruction*. After its success they re-released first single "Welcome to the Jungle" and didn't look back.

The band went on to sell more than one hundred million records, despite only releasing four full-length studio albums. Epic hard-rock tracks like "Don't Cry" and "November Rain" would cement them a place in music history, while Axl Rose's increasingly erratic behavior was equally infamous.

After a fifteen-year break between LPs and a vastly altered line-up, GN'R released its eagerly anticipated album, *Chinese Democracy*, in 2008, which, despite receiving mixed reviews, rocketed to the Top 5 on both sides of the Atlantic.

SWEET CHILD O' MINE   OUT TA GET ME / ROCKET QUEEN

Sweetest Thing

U2

Alison Stewart and Paul Hewson were teenage sweethearts. Their relationship goes back to their early-1970s schooldays at Dublin's Mount Temple Comprehensive School, where U2 was formed. Legend has it that Bono (as Hewson became known) unsuccessfully tried to chat up Alison on her first day at the school. Undaunted, he continued to pursue her, and according to Ali, "It was 1976 that we got together—the same year that the band formed. I saw their first gig, in our school gym.

Bono and Ali get collared for a comment backstage at Steve Wozniak's pioneering US Festival in San Bernardino, California, May 1983.

He was my first real boyfriend." Prior to this, after Bono's mother died in November 1974, Ali had looked after the less than practically minded singer, doing his laundry and cooking for him.

U2 were still an up-and-coming rock band with two albums behind them when Ali and Bono were married in August 1982 in Dublin. International renown followed the multiplatinum *The Joshua Tree* in 1987. "Sweetest Thing" was written by Bono as a present for Ali when he forgot her birthday while working on the album. The gift remained tucked away as a single B-side, until it was resurrected and reworked eleven years later. The Edge, U2's guitarist, explained why: "When we recorded *The Joshua Tree* we liked it, but it was her song so it was different from the rest. Afterwards we realized it should have been on the album."

Ali and Bono photographed at Saks on Fifth Avenue in New York at the launch of Edun, a "conscious commerce" clothing line, in March 2005.

The lyrics celebrate the contrasting characters of Bono and Ali, as well as the ups and downs of their enduring partnership.

> Baby's got blue skies up ahead
> But in this I'm a rain cloud
> You know she wants a dry kind of love

Ali's early ambition to become a nurse did not materialize; she worked in insurance and in her father's electrical business while the band struggled in the 1970s. In 1989 she graduated with a bachelor of arts in sociology and political science at University College Dublin, not long after the birth of the couple's first daughter, Jordan. Their second child, Eve, was born in 1991.

She appeared in the video for "Sweetest Thing," and the income she received for that was donated to the Chernobyl Children's Project International, a charity of which she is a patron. She has campaigned against the expansion of the U.K. nuclear plant at Sellafield and for Greenpeace. Having cofounded Nude, a company specialising in organic skincare, she followed up with Edun, an ethical fashion label.

Although she shares ecological and political beliefs with Bono, Ali strives to maintain her independence. "I hate being called 'Bono's wife,' and being identified just as that. I know that people who know me well enough don't think of me like that. But there are always going to be others who don't see me as having a separate identity, who just see us as the one person. At the end of the day, I don't really care what people think, just so long as I feel strong enough about myself."

The Hewsons are that rarest of things—the lasting rock star marriage. They still live in Ireland, at Killiney on the southern coast of County Dublin. Ali has no doubt as to the reasons why their marriage has succeeded through all the temptations that stardom and riches supply. "Knowing someone's memories is when you really know them inside out—when you've grown up with them and made that journey through adulthood together. It's about having respect for each other—allowing each other the space to grow and respecting that growth."

U2 and their expansive rock have been selling out arenas for more than three decades, racking up (at last count) nine U.K. #1 albums and an astonishing 22 Grammys along the way.

"Sweetest Thing" was originally the B-side to the band's 1987 Top 5 hit, "Where the Streets Have No Name," but was released as a single in its own right in 1998. By this point the band was known the world over, and the song made #3 in the U.K., though it failed to break the Billboard Top 40. It also appeared on the compilation album *The Best of U2* 1980-1990. A version of the song appears on the soundtrack to the 1988 Bill Murray film *Scrooged*, performed by the New Voices of Freedom.

Tiny Dancer
Elton John

She was the inspiration for one of Elton John's 1970s hits, but Maxine Feibelman was not romantically interested in the British superstar. Instead it was longtime lyricist and songwriting partner Bernie Taupin who held a place in her heart. It was Taupin who penned the track "Tiny Dancer" about Feibelman in 1970, after she had joined him and John on tour in the role of seamstress. As a trained dancer she would spend most of the shows at the side of the stage, dancing her way through the uptempo numbers. The lyrics tell the story of Taupin's feeling for his partner, predicting his marriage to his first wife:

> Blue jean baby, L.A. lady, seamstress for the band
> Pretty eyed, pirate smile, you'll marry a music man

He would eventually marry Feibelman in 1971—the same year the single was released, reaching #41 in the Billboard Hot 100. The wedding took place in his home village of Market Rasen in Lincolnshire. He'd been living there a few short years earlier when he answered a music-paper advertisement from a music company seeking a lyric writer. His pre-music jobs had ranged from farmhand to newspaper print operator. The local paper covered the ceremony in suitably gushing style.

"Bernie Taupin (21), remembered not so long ago as a rather shy and unassertive Market Rasen schoolboy, returned to the town again on Saturday as the songwriting hero of the pop world who was marrying a sweet girl from Los Angeles—who arrived at the Holy Rood Roman Catholic Church in a lilac-colored Aston Martin.

"The marriage service of Bernard John Taupin, of Owmby, and Maxine Feibelman, of Los Angeles, lost nothing of its solemnity ... (though) the eye-catching quality of male attire at this wedding meant that for once the bride, in her simple Tudor-style dress, did not stand out as the central figure in the ceremony. Bernie wore a white velvet suit, a lilac shirt and earrings. Elton John, Bernie's pop-star partner, was also in white as the best man, outshining all Rasen best men who ever were.

"In the congregation were familiar figures of the world of pop, giving the scene an appearance of showbiz unreality."

Two days later, instead of flying out for an exotic honeymoon, the couple flew back to Los Angeles for an Elton John tour. It was Maxine Taupin who gave Bernie the idea for the lyrics to Elton's 1974 hit, "The Bitch Is Back." Fed up with one too many tantrums from Elton and hearing him ranting about anything and everything, she turned to Bernie and said, "Uh oh, the bitch is back." Bernie wrote the lyric and Elton happily sang the self-mocking song.

One of the few showbiz weddings where the best man outshone the bride.

But Taupin could not make it work with his new American wife; his reported drink issues and love of the rock 'n' roll lifestyle saw the couple divorce just five years later in 1976. While Maxine would slip out of the public eye, Taupin would go on to find love—and heartbreak—with Toni Lynn Russo (1979), sister of actress Rene, and Stephanie Haymes (1993), before marrying Heather Lynn Hodgins Kidd (2004).

ELTON JOHN released "Tiny Dancer" as only his fifth single. It was taken from the album *Madman Across the Water*, which appeared in a rush of early album releases, between 1970 and 1971, that cashed in on his immediate U.S. impact: *Elton John*, *Tumbleweed Connection*, *17-11-70*, *Madman Across the Water*, and the soundtrack to the movie *Friends* and 1969's *Empty Sky* were testaments to a prolific talent.

The song enjoyed a new lease on life in 2009, when rapper DJ Ironik used it as the musical basis for his hit with Chipmunk, "Tiny Dancer (Hold Me Closer)."

John's follow-up album in 1972, *Honky Château*, went straight in at #1 in the U.K., while narrowly missing out on the top spot in America. The less successful *Madman Across the Water* was but a blip in an otherwise stellar career.

Turn Your Lights Down Low

Bob Marley

Bob Marley ruled the world of reggae for two decades. In that time he took it from the fringes of popular music into the mainstream, where it would remain long after his death in 1981.

As well as his musical talent, Marley was known for his love of marijuana and women. Despite being married to wife Rita from 1966 till his untimely death, Marley had a number of extramarital affairs, leading to eleven officially recognized children by seven different women, with more undoubtedly existing off the record.

But there was one woman who touched Marley more than most: her name was Cindy Breakspeare, aka Miss Jamaica. The two reportedly began their relationship shortly

Cindy Breakspeare with Bob Marley in Kingston, 1980, a year before his death.

before the Canadian-born model won Miss World in 1976, becoming only the third Jamaican to do so.

As long-suffering Rita turned a blind eye to her husband's newest affair, Marley and sometime-musician Breakspeare's relationship flourished. "I knew from the first time that I ever spoke with him," she commented, "that a deep relationship would change my life permanently. I knew that."

She recalled the time she first heard the track he had penned for her. "He would sit on the steps out the back of my apartment there with a guitar and sing. I remember hearing "Turn Your Lights Down Low" just like that. He wasn't a man of words on a one-to-one basis, you know, not a lot, and certainly not when he was just getting to know somebody; he was very shy that way."

Their relationship continued and culminated in the birth of a son, Damien, in 1978. Shortly afterwards the pair drifted apart, as Marley went to stay in Miami to help boost his rising U.S. career, while Breakspeare stayed in Jamaica with Damien.

The couple remained friends, as Breakspeare explained. "It was never an official situation where I said, 'Look, it's over,' or he said, 'Look, it's over.' It was just more or less a situation where he'd gone up to Miami to prepare to go out on tour, and I decided I wanted to move away from [Kingston], because I felt like I needed some space. So I found a small place in the hills that was just big enough for Damien and I."

Marley passed away from cancer three years later in 1981, but he kept in contact with Breakspeare up until the end. She married attorney Tom Tavares-Finson, also in 1981, and had two children with him, Christian in 1982 and Leah in 1986. She continued to make music and remarried, this time a musician, Rupert Bent.

But she still looks back fondly on her time with the king of reggae. "He was very charismatic, very strong and I always have liked that in people in general, and in particular in the men that I choose to spend time with."

With Damien Marley now a Grammy Award–winning reggae artist in his own right, "Turn Your Lights Down Low" could be said to be an important song in extending father Bob's legacy even further after his death.

BOB MARLEY pioneered reggae music and brought it to the world at large. Though his life was ended prematurely by cancer, he did enough in his thirty-six years to have his name permanently attached to the genre.

Marley and backing group the Wailers released the album *Exodus* in 1977. It included "Turn Your Lights Down Low," and one of Marley's biggest hits, "Jammin'."

The album hit #20 in the U.S. and #8 in the U.K. Four years later Marley would pass away, but his last studio LP, *Uprising,* reached the U.K. Top 10. He has enjoyed posthumous success with tracks like "Buffalo Soldier."

"Turn Your Lights Down Low" was covered by Fugees singer Lauryn Hill, who is the mother of five children with Bob's fourth son, Rohan Marley.

Under My Thumb
The Rolling Stones

It was January 1963. The Rolling Stones' line-up was complete—Charlie Watts had just been recruited on drums, and Bill Wyman joined the band on bass the previous month. Already they had secured a Sunday residency at the legendary Crawdaddy Club in Richmond. They were also booked to play the Ricky Tick Club at the Thames Hotel in Windsor, and it was here that Chrissie Shrimpton introduced herself to Mick Jagger in unorthodox fashion.

Chrissie was the wild younger sister of photographer David Bailey's favorite model, Jean Shrimpton. She became the subject of several Stones hits both during and after her stormy three-year relationship with Mick Jagger—a relationship which ended abruptly just before Christmas in 1966.

Clambering onto a table in the bar of the Thames Hotel, Chrissie pulled herself up into the fishing nets which decorated the ceiling of the room. Then, with the help of the audience below, who passed her along with their hands as if she were a crowd surfer, she worked her way along until she was above the stage. Lowering herself down, she then walked over to Jagger and kissed him full on those Rolling Stone lips in front of everybody.

The young Mick Jagger was, metaphorically at least, swept off his feet. Romance blossomed quickly, and within weeks Jagger had made the first of several proposals of marriage to her. She was the first girl he took home to meet his parents, and they approved of her. As late as June 1965 there were rumors of their impending wedding, but in truth the relationship was already in terminal decline.

Drugs played a central role, as one might expect, in the relationship of a couple at the very center of swinging London in the early 1960s. It was a time when many substances had yet to be declared illegal. At first neither was fully aware of the extent of the other's consumption, but at some point they shared their first acid trip, an event commemorated in the lyrics of "19th Nervous Breakdown." It was a bad trip for Chrissie, inducing bouts of paranoia and triggering a steady mental decline.

Returning home from a vacation in the Caribbean in 1965. A year later things would be much less sunny.

Jagger for his part was notoriously possessive and controlling. In 2004 Shrimpton, then fifty-eight, recalled that he would pay her bar bills, but only on condition she returned home from the nightclub when he ordered her to. "He would often phone up, and I was told I had to go home now ... and he would ring at home at three in the morning. I kind of liked that." The years may have softened her memories—on at least one occasion she was so agitated at Jagger's late return that she set about him with her fists when he came in. He fled.

Aftermath, the LP which followed the hit single "19th Nervous Breakdown" in April 1966, contained at least two more songs about Chrissie Shrimpton. "Under My Thumb" is a hymn to male domination and seems to be suggesting that Jagger has finally tamed the wild assertive girl. He had turned "the squirming dog" into "the sweetest pet."

Another song from *Aftermath* inspired by Chrissie, "Stupid Girl," is nothing more than a list of schoolboy insults and attacks. Shrimpton's obvious inability to handle the unstable 1960s mix of sex, drugs, and rock 'n' roll must have been frustrating for Jagger, who took it all in stride. In August 1966 the pair escaped serious injury in a road accident that wrecked Jagger's Aston Martin DB6 sportscar. The relationship, too, was heading for the scrapyard. Toward the end of the year Jagger, who had started an affair with Marianne Faithfull, decided to end it with Chrissie Shrimpton. At first though, he didn't tell her, and he expressed surprise

London, 1968: Chrissie Shrimpton was able to return to her career in modeling after her time with Jagger, but she never reached the heights of more famous sister Jean.

when Chrissie complained that the Rolling Stones office (acting in fact on his orders) had stopped paying her bar bills.

On December 15 Mick and Chrissie were due to fly to Jamaica for Christmas, but instead Mick spent the day shopping at Harrods with Marianne. It was the last straw. Three days later, after one final screaming match, Shrimpton tried to take her life with an overdose of sleeping pills. Medics saved her life and pumped her stomach. Jagger got the bill and refused to pay it. Instead he issued a statement announcing merely that his relationship with Shrimpton was over, and that "I don't dig the marriage bit at the moment." He then had all her possessions boxed and taken away from his London apartment. It was Christmas Eve.

Two weeks later, to add insult to injury, "Let's Spend the Night Together" became a massive transatlantic hit. It had been written after Jagger's first night with Faithfull. Chrissie, on the rebound, started a short-lived affair with Steve Marriott of the Small Faces; the couple was detained on suspicion of possessing drugs in February.

When that relationship fizzled out three months later, Marriott wrote "Talk to You," the B-side of the Small Faces' hit "Here Comes the Nice," which was about losing Shrimpton. Jagger in turn penned the cruel dismissal, "Yesterday's Papers," complete with put-downs such as, "Who wants yesterday's papers? Who wants yesterday's girl?"

Chrissie Shrimpton subsequently appeared in a handful of films, most notably George Lazenby's ill-fated project *Universal Soldier* in 1971. Since then she has disappeared from public view.

THE ROLLING STONES are one of the most successful rock 'n' roll bands in history, their peak coming with a run of eight consecutive #1 albums in America during the 1970s and 1980s. The song "19th Nervous Breakdown" was released as a single in 1966, reaching #2 in the U.S. "Under My Thumb" was a track on 1966's *Aftermath,* while "Yesterday's Papers," also an album cut, appeared on the following year's *Between the Buttons.* In December 2003, Mick Jagger was knighted for his services to music.

Uptown Girl
Billy Joel

A s any golden oldies DJ will tell you, "Uptown Girl" is a guaranteed floor filler with those of a certain age, right up there with Abba's "Dancing Queen" and "YMCA" by the Village People. And no wonder—it has a strong musical pedigree. Billy Joel had been honing his craft as a pop musician since 1964, when he saw the Beatles on *The Ed Sullivan Show* and decided he wanted to follow their example.

The forty-year career that followed is a testament to his talent, of course, but also to sheer hard work. For five long years he played in covers bands, learning all there is to know about what makes a pop song a hit. When at the height of his success in 1983 he came to record the album *An Innocent Man*, he wanted to make it an affectionate nod to the roots of pop music, the rock 'n' roll of his early days as a musician.

With "Uptown Girl" he recreated and updated the infectious rhythms and harmonies of Frankie Valli and the Four Seasons, a mix that worked as well for him as it had done for Frankie and the boys.

Joel wrote the song at a time when he was enjoying an energetic new lease on life. He was a rock star at the top of his game and recently single (his first marriage had just ended in divorce); he was flying high and determined to make the most of his situation. The lyrics describe not one but two romantic conquests he made in the process.

While vacationing in the Caribbean, he found that among the fellow guests in his hotel was a group of fashion models who had gathered to do a magazine shoot. They included the soon-to-be-famous Whitney Houston and already-very-famous supermodels Christie Brinkley and Elle Macpherson.

Joel, a short, stocky ex-boxer from New York, claims he was able to attract the attention of such glamorous women by the power of music alone (although one may suspect that being a famous pop star also had something to do with it). He was playing the piano in the hotel bar one evening, when "I looked up and there were these three gorgeous women looking at me from the other side of the piano. I looked back down at the piano and just said 'Thank you.'"

It was Elle Macpherson that he began to date, and about whom he started to write the song. Australian Elle would later achieve lasting fame as only the second model to appear on three consecutive covers of *Sports Illustrated* magazine's annual Swimsuit Issue (1986–1988). The first person to complete this hat trick was none other than Christie Brinkley (1979–1981), and after his romance with Macpherson ended Billy started dating her. When that relationship began to get serious, Billy shrewdly dropped the "s" from the song's original title, "Uptown Girls."

Christie appeared in the video for "Uptown Girl" (as the girl in the car attended to by mechanic Billy). The couple wed in 1985, and their marriage endured longer than many do in the strained world of showbiz relationships. Brinkley and Joel divorced in 1994 but remained on good enough terms for him to be a guest at her fourth wedding in 1996—and she in return attended his third in 2004. By 2009 both were single again.

Christie Brinkley has managed the tricky transition from calendar girl to businessperson, lending

In the 1980s, Billy Joel's little black book—which included Elle Macpherson—was more like the credits for **Sports Illustrated** *swimsuit issues.*

her name to a wide range of health, beauty, and fitness products. She also campaigns for animal rights, vegetarianism, and the antinuclear lobby; since 1998 she has been a prominent contributor to the Democratic Party.

Her artwork is on the cover of Joel's 1993 album, *River of Dreams*, his last collection of new pop material. It includes "Lullabye (Goodnight, My Angel)," written for their daughter Alexa Ray Joel. Disillusioned with the music industry, Joel announced soon after its release his intention to stop writing pop. His efforts as a composer since then have been works for classical piano and orchestra.

Daughter Alexa has struggled, like so many celebrity offspring, to find her own place in the world. High-achieving parents are a hard act to follow. In 2006 she began performing as a singer-songwriter in her own right and released a six-song EP. She toured steadily, but a failed love affair with the bassist in her band triggered a prolonged bout of depression, which strangely echoed an unhappy episode in her father's life.

During two dark periods (2009 for her, 1970 for him), they were both struggling to get their musical careers off the ground and both despondent in the wake of broken love affairs. Both attempted suicide in tragicomic circumstances. Billy tried to overdose on lemon-scented furniture polish, which he chose because it was marked with a skull and crossbones and "looked tastier than bleach." The result, he commented later, was merely some fragrant breaking of wind. Alexa swallowed eight

BILLY JOEL worked tirelessly over his career to become the third biggest selling solo artist in the U.S. His middle-of-the-road piano rock and ballads have enabled him to maintain his success for more than forty years. "Uptown Girl" was a #1 hit for Joel in the U.K. on its release in 1983. It hit #3 in the Billboard Hot 100, and the album that carried the track, *An Innocent Man*, reached #4 in the U.S. Joel released further LPs, two of which—*Storm Front* and *River of Dreams*—topped the U.S. album charts in 1989 and 1993 respectively. He continues to tour today.

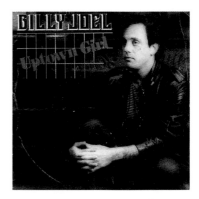

pills of a low-concentration homeopathic antihistamine, which a toxicologist declared would be almost impossible to overdose on. It was, however, an undeniable cry for help.

Luckily for all concerned, neither father nor daughter suffered lasting damage, and both careers took an upturn soon after. Billy's is well documented; Alexa's music has been chosen for a 2010 shampoo advertising campaign, of which she is also the face. It's a happier echo, this time of something in her mother's career—Christie Brinkley was the face in TV commercials for the same shampoo when it was first launched twenty-four years earlier.

The second uptown girl. Joel has notched up three marriages, Christie Brinkley four. Now their daughter Alexa is trying to follow her father into the music business.

Wonderwall
Oasis

M eg Mathews was introduced to Noel Gallagher in November 1994 by her flatmate, MTV Europe host Rebecca de Ruvo. Gallagher feared that he had not made a good first impression and that Meg considered him a "miserable wanker." He had just been asked to leave his Chiswick flat because of his "recreational activities" and, to make matters worse, his soccer team, Manchester City, had suffered a heavy defeat against local rivals United the day before. Despite this they quickly became friends and subsequently lovers, as Meg explains.

"When I first met Noel we lived in (Smiths guitarist) Johnny Marr's flat near Blakes Hotel in Roland Gardens, South Kensington. It was beautiful, and a great address, but it was a temporary setup. Noel and I moved in together just two weeks after meeting. We soon found our own little flat in Camden. It was tiny and pretty basic but we were in love so it didn't matter. It was rock 'n' roll. People like Bono would just drop in."

Matthews had a profound effect on Gallagher despite some negative first impressions.

Meg's impact on Noel's life was immediate; she took over his social diary and helped change his taste in clothes from brands like Fred Perry and Lacoste to the more upmarket designer labels Gucci and Prada.

Born in Guernsey and raised in Durban, South Africa, Mathews later attended boarding school in Norfolk before hitching alone to London at nineteen. Nine years later, she had worked her way up from selling wigs on Kensington Market to running a DJ-booking agency, via a stint as personal assistant to early-1990s pop singer Betty Boo. When she first encountered Noel Gallagher, his band Oasis was about to change the indie-rock rule book and branch out firmly into the mainstream. Their first album, *Definitely Maybe*, consisting entirely of Noel's songs, had already become the fastest-selling debut by a British group.

"Wonderwall," a ballad representing a change in direction for Oasis, was released in November 1995, a year after Meg and Noel first got together. Noel explained the inspiration behind the song while previewing the band's second album in *Loaded* magazine shortly before it debuted. "It's about my girlfriend," he said, "because she had just lost her job and didn't have any money and all the rest of it." Meg quickly became famous as half of one of Brit-pop's most famous couples after Noel's gruff declaration of love, and the song enjoyed a lengthy run in the singles chart.

Mathews and Gallagher were fixtures of the scene now dubbed "Cool Britannia" and regulars in the tabloid press. Meg in particular had a reputation as a party girl, hanging out in the most fashionable places with celebrity friends such as model Kate Moss and designer Stella McCartney. "Being thrust into the limelight as a young girl from Norfolk was really amazingly difficult, too," says Mathews. "I can see that with hindsight; though at the time I guess I was blind to it." At the same time, she admitted that, "I was having a great time. I loved every minute of it."

They were married in Las Vegas in June 1997, to the accompaniment of Beatles songs and entertainment provided by an Elvis impersonator. In late 2000, eight months after the birth of their daughter Anais, they split up and were divorced in January 2001. Ostensibly, Noel took the blame, admitting to adultery with publicist Sara MacDonald, who was to become his long-term partner.

In 2006, Meg checked into rehab, emerging calmer and with a new zeal for health and fitness. Since then, she has founded a design company.

OASIS is one of the most successful British rock 'n' roll bands of a generation. Brothers Noel and Liam Gallagher fronted a group that helped revolutionize British music in the 1990s. "Wonderwall" has become arguably their most recognizable song since it was released in 1995. It featured on the band's second album, *(What's the Story) Morning Glory*, which became their biggest success both in the U.K. and in America, selling more than twenty-two million copies across the world. The brothers' volatile relationship was as much a selling point for the group as it was a hindrance on their future. The band split up in 2009 after seven studio albums.

I Acknowledgments

Acknowledgments

Thanks to Mike Gent, Drew Heatley and Colin Salter for additional research; Kate Saunders from BBC Radio 4 for the Suzanne Verdal interview, and Emily Young for gently pointing out that her sculpture was no longer in Kew Gardens.